The REALITY *of*

(BIG SALES, THAT IS!)

STEVEN O. HOFFMAN

THE REALITY OF BS
(BIG SALES, THAT IS!)

iUniverse books may be ordered through booksellers or by contacting:

iUniverse
1663 Liberty Drive
Bloomington, IN 47403
www.iuniverse.com
1-800-Authors (1-800-288-4677)

ISBN: 978-1-5320-8329-7 (sc)
ISBN: 978-1-5320-8328-0 (e)

Library of Congress Control Number: 2019914141

Print information available on the last page.

iUniverse rev. date: 10/30/2019

This book is dedicated to Ellen Hoffman

Without a doubt, you are the best deal I ever closed.

Contents

Part 3 - Sales Fallacies

Part 4 - Selling Like Your Career Depends On It

The How, Why & When of This Book

On the Border
Greenville, SC
New Year's Eve

The tide was turning in the battle for our family to get a dog. With the kids now won over, it was three-to-one with my wife being the lone hold-out. Somewhere between chips and guacamole and the check arriving, we struck a deal that led to this book.

I had been talking about writing a book on sales for years. Instead of "put-up or shut-up," the deal was if I wrote the book and submitted it for publication by the next New Year's Eve, we could get a dog. Casper, our Maltese, joined the family on Halloween later that year.

But then life got in the way of agents, publishers and necessary revisions. I wound up buying, relaunching and continuing to grow a portion of the company that is referenced many times in the following pages. In the ensuing years, when doing a training session or speaking in public, someone would often say to me, "you should write a book."

Little did they know it was already written. But surely, whatever was written a decade and a half back would no longer be relevant? Or would it?

In the spring of 2019, I attended an advanced sales training class. This was the type of high dollar training often aimed at big corporations with big training budgets. It featured pre-class survey testing, workbooks with charts... lots of charts. There were presentations and role playing and post-course analysis that included, yes – even more charts.

When compiling my notes from the course to share with my team, I ignored the charts and convoluted descriptions and focused on distilling the best of the important concepts I had taken away. So much of what was in my summary reminded me of the concepts I had written about many years before. And then, in a follow-up conversation, one of the course's instructors suggested that I write a book.

The Reality of BS is a collection of things that should be important to a sales professional at any stage of their career. Sharing lessons through stories is a lesson unto itself: Most of you are selling to adults and one of the ways adults remember concepts is via storytelling.

The stories that follow share lessons learned, often the hard way. Many of the stories are from earlier in my career, but the lessons are pertinent and will remain important to sales professionals for years to come.

Many names of individuals (and a few companies) in these true stories have been changed to protect their privacy. My hope is some of these "tales of the sale" will make you laugh, but more importantly, I hope you'll be able to recall a lesson or two when you might need them. After all, if a sales rep, manager or business owner is going to take the time to read a book, they better be able to take some things out of it that make it worth their time!

PART 1

Setting The Sale

The Hooker And The Sales Smorgasbord

Seedy Side of Town
Anywhere, USA
The Oldest Profession

There's an old joke that goes like this: a man walks up to a provocatively dressed, sleazy but sexy woman. She is leaning on a streetlight in a part of town known for prostitution. He asks, "Would you go to bed with me for a million bucks?"

The woman replies, "For a million bucks, of course." The man, let's call him "John," then asks, "Well, would you go to bed with me for a dollar?" To this, the hooker adamantly says, "For a dollar? No way! What do you think I am?" The "John" answers, "Well, we know what you are. Now we're just haggling over price."

Sales, as a profession or an action, is as diverse as the world around us. Writing a book about sales, salespeople and their activities is necessarily challenged by the diversity among us. There are salespeople who sell ideas and salespeople who sell products.

Just as retail sales experiences differ for the consumer (i.e., shopping on Main St. in a rural town versus shopping on Worth Avenue in Palm Beach), so do business-to-business transactions. While retail sales is a very different discipline from B-to-B, retail sales professionals may find that many of the sales basics addressed in the following chapters can be adapted to fit their situations, too.

Not only does business-to-business selling differ from retail, but B-to-B differs from B-to-C, or business to consumer selling. Within the scope of B-to-B selling, the actions, requirements and skills needed will vary greatly according to industry, product, sales cycle, methodology and the target customer base. And of course, E-commerce disrupts everything.

This book necessarily cannot be all things to all people. So, who will benefit from *The Reality of BS?* The young person investigating future careers will come across some realities they don't teach in school (and some they should). The novice salesperson early in their career who is fighting to get ahead in this ever-changing profession of ours can immediately implement many of the tactics. And the veteran sales rep will be thankful for the reminders of what they once knew.

And of course, I benefit, too. After all, you bought the book!

Dinner With Doctors And Lawyers

The Oyster Bar
Grand Central Station, NYC

I met my brother the lawyer for lunch. It was rare that we'd get together in the middle of a workday, but I had big news and wanted to celebrate, especially if he was paying. Group W Television (a division of Westinghouse) had just offered me a sales position.

It was the third stop in my sales career since graduating from college. Both previous positions were also in the television program syndication business. The first job was with D.L. Taffner/Ltd. where, like many degreed college graduates in the entertainment industry, I started in the mail room. Over the course of a few years I moved through the research and promotions departments.

Hotshot salespeople at that time were heading to Wall Street. My company sold "re-runs" of sitcoms. They dealt in commodities, futures, stocks and bonds. We distributed "Three's Company" and "Benny Hill." My position evolved into a station relations role whereby I became a support person to the salespeople.

The Reps had nicer clothes and took better vacations. Their paychecks were bigger. They were the guys who made it happen. That was what I wanted to be doing. Without any near-term prospects of an opening within Taffner, I applied for a position with Syndicast Services. They needed a promotion assistant with a research background and were willing to give me sales responsibilities, too.

The product was still TV programming, but instead of well-known sitcom hits we sold lots of "O-T-O's" (one-time-only specials), ranging from beauty pageants to kids' programs and documentaries. When the company was purchased by Australian investors, it led to new product developments including a first run movie, a daily health and fitness show with Richard Simmons, and a wonderful but short-lived political puppet show called *D.C. Follies*.

This was what my brother knew of my background when we met for lunch. He, the lawyer. Me, on the fringes of an industry where some folks made lots of money, but most just worked hard, did their jobs and were never touched by fame or fortune. He was happy for me but rightly concerned for my future, and our discussion eventually turned to money.

While I don't remember my exact salary, it was double or more what I'd been making previously. What I do remember and will never forget is both his expression and his words, "Wow, I didn't know salespeople could make that much!"

Skyline Displays
Training Room - Burnsville, MN

Following an early mid-life crisis that left me with a burning desire to leave my native NY and head south, my family and I found ourselves in Greenville, South Carolina. I had left television and entered the tradeshow marketing industry, taking a job with the local distributor for a well-known exhibit manufacturer.

To their credit, Skyline Exhibits (formerly Skyline Displays) has always invested in training its worldwide sales force. While their 'Skyline University' program has been through many evolutions, the basic commitment to having the best trained reps in the industry has been a constant.

My first visit to Skyline was for their "Sky U 101" course. At that time, Stan Piedrick was the VP of Sales & Marketing and he personally conducted much of the training. Prior to Skyline, Stan had sold for a custom display house and been a college professor.

The group consisted of rookie reps from all over the world with a wide array of backgrounds and sales experience. Piedrick walked us through preliminaries and logistics of the three-day training. Then, he talked about why he liked sales.

He talked about his big new house. He talked about his new car. He mentioned how there was a sense of security that came with sales because he could control or influence his income, and with three small children, that was important.

He went on to discuss his friends, saying that many of them were doctors and lawyers. And, addressing all of us rookie reps, he said that we could have incomes on par with our doctor and lawyer buddies. There was no disdain for lesser compensated individuals. There was no false bravado. It was pure, encouraging fact.

I believe Stan went on to join an internet start-up in the midst of the dot. com craze. So now he's either very wealthy, or somewhere in that big house he has wallpaper made from worthless stock options.

Skyline has been through numerous Sales Manager/VP types in the 25 years I've been affiliated with them since starting at The Oliver Group, their Carolina distributor. I'll always remember Piedrick for that speech and for one other thing. Stan was the first person to whom I ever attempted to send an e-mail. I accidentally hit send when it was only half written and what I sent was ripe for either legal, ethical or business backlash. We all learn from our mistakes!

Khaki's
Greenville, South Carolina

As a teenager I worked at a summer camp for underprivileged kids. I was too young to be hired at most places, but through a neighbor I had the opportunity to be a life guard and a Junior Counselor. As a white Jew from the suburbs, spending a few summers where I was a minority amongst the mostly Black and Hispanic staff and campers was a learning experience.

Beyond the more important lessons that would serve me throughout life and career were some wonderful ways to describe 'altered states of reality.' I remember five of us counselors lying on a hillside one night, just beyond the camp fence, hanging out and staring at the moon. Whether it was the cheap wine, the cheaper beer, or the sickeningly sweet mixed concoctions, everyone was feeling fine (and at least one or two were old enough to be drinking).

Food was in order. Someone had a car and being the responsible caretakers of young children that we were (although the kids were asleep in the bunks), someone inquired as to whether the driver was drunk. With the most relaxed, sincere smile emanating from his white teeth set against his dark skin glowing in the middle of the night, he said "no man, I'm not drunk. I'm just *NICE*."

Thirty years later my wife and I attend a cocktail party. The hosts were a couple we knew through our Temple. They were comparable in age with us. That particular evening, our small town had both a touring company for a Broadway show and an Eric Clapton concert.

Many of the party guests headed out from the party early to attend one or the other of these events. The rest of us relaxed, had a few more cocktails and went to dinner. I have a wonderful wife who is either cursed or blessed (depending on your outlook) with an allergy to alcohol. Our hosts lived in a huge custom-restored home on a mountain just minutes from the city. It had gorgeous views and was accessible only through a narrow windy road.

Knowing my wife would have the "down the mountain" driving chores under control and that we were leaving on vacation the next day, I felt a particular obligation to assist several of our friends in not letting the last batch of Margaritas, or Gimlets, or "house specials" go to waste before we went to dinner.

Five couples, a table for ten and I wound up at one of the "heads" or ends of the table. Another drink. I remember thinking back to what Stan Piedrick had said about salespeople and being able to keep up with the Doctors and Lawyers. Immediately to my right was a good friend, an attorney, with his own practice. Our hosts from earlier in the evening were both doctors. And next to them sat another doctor.

I wasn't drunk. I was just feeling NICE!

How Many Sales Did It Take To Get This Book In Your Hands?

The initial answer of "only one – I went to a bookstore or clicked purchase' and they gave me the book" is incorrect. Think about this:

First, the author had to be sold on the idea of doing a book. Then, the book idea had to be sold to an agent who had to sell it to a publishing house. The publishers had to sell it to distributors who sold it to retailers. Then, you came along.

But that's not all. It's a good bet you were wearing clothing when you went to the bookstore. Someone sold those clothes to you. The company that made the clothing purchased raw materials as well as equipment, their telephone system, health insurance and marketing support for their staff. Those products and services were all sold.

How did you get to the store to buy this book? Did someone sell you a car that was utilized? A single car uses thousands of parts all of which get sold to the manufacturer. Did you buy the book online? Who sold you the computer? Who sold that website their servers and software?

Before the book in your hands was in its present form, it was a tree! Someone sold the land to a timber company who also bought lots of equipment and chemicals to grow healthy trees so their owners could sell the trees and then buy nice things from other salespeople. The sales reps for the timber company sold the trees to paper processing mills who in turn sell paper to printers and binders.

The book in your hands would be a bunch of blank pages were it not for the fact that someone sold the printer ink. Historically, too, printers were good accounts for soap salesmen.

Did you hear about the book on a TV or radio station where advertising time gets sold to companies that are trying to sell you their products and services? Did you just start thumbing through the book while at the bookstore and decide to read a few pages in one of their comfortable chairs?

That chair was sold to the bookstore. The chair's manufacturer bought fabric, wood, springs and stuffing all purchased from different salespeople. From still other sales reps they bought machinery to make the chair to make you comfortable. To keep track of it all they worked with accountants and lawyers who sold them services.

Did you buy a coffee while in the bookstore? In a jungle in Colombia someone sold the land to grow the beans and onward straight through to your latte and the cup it's in.

Without salespeople, nothing happens.

PART 2

Making The Sale

Rule #1 – You Don't Ask, You Don't Get

Group W TV Sales
New York City

More often than we think about it, the thing that we need to sell is ourselves. If a prospect doesn't like us, trust us, feel comfortable with us and/or believe we can help them, why would they want to do business with us?

In a job interview situation, where you are literally 'selling yourself,' these same considerations apply. Similarly, if the potential employee is strong the company should be conscious about how it sells itself. Some companies have reputations that create a desire for people to want to work there.

Such was the case when Westinghouse needed a NY-based rep to cover the Southeast. My work with Syndicast had given me the necessary background to apply. Seven interviews later I found myself in the office of Ned Goldstein, President of Group W TV Sales.

Like me, Ned was a New York Jewish guy. One of his memorable questions dealt with how I'd bridge the cultural gap of being a New Yorker and selling to Southerners.

Virtually every salesperson has to address a cultural gap many times in their careers. Perhaps some of you can benefit from what I told Ned that day.

To fully appreciate the situation, you should know that we were in a Manhattan Skyscraper about 50 floors over Park Avenue. Ned had the corner office. It was large, impressive and maybe a little intimidating to an interviewee.

As we looked out of the floor-to-ceiling glass windows, I struggled for the words to let him know that I agreed that many New Yorkers were full of themselves and the "superior than thou" attitude had to be left at LaGuardia. I went on to babble something about treating all people with respect and not to make assumptions about anyone you'd meet with.

It helped, too, that I had already been successfully selling to the same client base this position would call for. I could offer numerous success stories as well as references. Thinking back on that day, I can't help but wonder if my camp counselor experiences fifteen years earlier, where I was a (white) fish out of water, played a role in preparing me for that interview, and the job that followed.

Throughout that interview we talked about mutual acquaintances. We discussed product development and plans for the division I'd be working with. Whether or not it was a conscious test of his at the time, there was *one thing* he wanted to make sure that any sales rep working for him knew.

Ned asked something along the lines of, "What do you do to get them to buy?" I'm sure my answer started with a bit of rambling. I then progressed to something along the lines of, "Get the customer to sell themselves on the benefits and realize how the product meets their needs."

The clincher was when I replied, "Of course, you have to ask for the order." The president's relief was palpable. I had hit on Ned Goldstein's first rule of salesmanship: "You don't ask, you don't get!"

If only we salespeople got every order we asked for! Having worked with, sold to, lectured to and consulted with thousands of salespeople, I know all of us can benefit from being sure our "techniques" include the basic step of "asking for the order."

Moreover, I see lots of sales left on the table because the rep doesn't educate the client on "how to buy." What a shame when a legitimate client need can be met by a company's product, but the rep doesn't assist them over the logistical purchasing hump.

I've utilized "Rule #1" in situations where absolutely nothing in the meeting that preceded my asking for the order warranted it and have been rewarded for doing so. I'm not suggesting a rep should ignore common sense, decorum, or other sales fundamentals, like not asking for the business until you understand the need or have created the value for your product or service. If the sales cycle doesn't lend itself to asking for the order, at the very least ask for the next step in the process.

"Rule #1" has also become a part of my repertoire during interviews with potential reps for our company. Not only do I want to be sure they know about asking a client for the order, but they must, ideally without prompting, demonstrate it by asking for the job.

Whether looking for that next order or your next sales position, always remember, "You don't ask, you don't get!"

Results Matter

Medstar Communications
Allentown, PA

I think I was fired.
If not, it's the closest I ever want to come.

My extensive travel in the Southeast with Group W solidified my desire to live there. Or, for that matter, anywhere but New York. Every sales rep should always have a concern with quality-of-life issues. I was living in Westchester County with an office in midtown Manhattan and clients spread around the country. I had a desire for "wholeness," for not having my life spread out. I was tired of airplanes and airports. I wanted my living room and a backyard.

Having already missed far too many moments of watching my son grow up, I was determined not to miss any more. But my wife was not yet ready to move South, so we compromised, and I accepted a position in Pennsylvania that would get me out of the city, into small town life and keep us within a close drive to her family.

Professionally, I was somewhat intrigued because the company that recruited me was distributing a TV Program called *Health Matters*. It incorporated many elements of what I'd been doing in the past (selling TV programming and TV program marketing packages) but also presented some new challenges. Specifically, the series needed to be sold twice – and then custom produced.

Of the two required sales, one was to a TV station to carry the show. The other sale required was to a hospital or health system to sponsor the series and provide the medical experts used in production of the local segments. The company also sold or syndicated local newscast medical inserts to TV stations.

One of the great lessons I learned from my time with Medstar was that a sales rep needs to look beyond their company and product to the industry as a whole and recognize how trends in that industry can and will affect sales. At that time, I failed to comprehend the paralyzing impact on marketing that would result from a tidal wave of change in the healthcare market.

Essentially, individual hospitals were being gobbled up by health system corporations. These same health systems were also buying up private physician practices. The goal was to cobble together a complete array of health services in order to enable the corporation to become a preferred provided to an insurance company's population of members. This represented a change from the traditional healthcare model of "fee-for-service" to the newer trend of "managed healthcare."

"Fee-for-service" meant doctors and hospitals wanted to treat people. That is, the more procedures they performed, the longer they could keep you in the hospital bed, and the more money they could make. Conversely, under "managed healthcare," insurance companies would pay a set fee to a health care provider (hospital or physician practice).

Albeit over-simplified, hospitals could make more money from not providing treatment because they'd already been paid to treat the "patient pool" when necessary. So, the less treatment they actually provided, the greater their profit would be.

Like so many trends in business and society, "managed care" was pervasive on the west coast before moving cross country. As it moved, people knew it was coming. Often before it got there, health systems were stymied about its impact on operations – including marketing.

I thought my first year at Medstar went fairly well. But I was measuring myself against the other National Account Manager (our title for sales rep). What I should have done – and what all reps should do – is have had a thorough understanding of both the management and owners' expectations.

I had grown close to Pedro Menedes, my sales manager at the time. Two particular lessons stand out. Pedro was insistent I take up golf, as it seemed both our owner and our clients were all golfers. I took one lesson. The next day I went to a driving range and literally (accidentally) let go of the club on my downswing, throwing the club about 105 yards while the ball trickled seven feet.

The next weekend I was convinced I was ready for a real golf course, so I tackled Allentown's municipal course. This was to practice for the next week's business trip to New Orleans. Pedro and I, along with two clients, played at the English Turn Golf and Country Club, at that time home of the New Orleans stop of the PGA tour.

Somewhere along those eighteen chances to demonstrate I was a complete beginner to the game of golf, I learned that in business golf, it's not so much the quality (nor quantity) of your score, but the character of the player that matters.

Pedro was also great in dealing with what I've come to call the "crisis du jour." Whether it was production problems with a job in progress, or sales problems with pursuit of an account, he'd be an aggressive listener, allowing the client to voice all issues, before voicing knee-jerk or patchwork solutions.

Not only was the medical world in transition, but the broadcast side of the business was also evolving. Before the days of Hulu and Netflix, even before cable systems or satellite providers offered 500 channels, television stations would air programs that were acquired in one of three ways. If a station was a network affiliate, they received a portion of their programming from the network. Stations (at that time mostly network affiliates) also locally produced some portion of their broadcast schedules. Mostly, this was local news. Whether an affiliate or an independent station, some or all of their schedules would be acquired from program syndicators.

Television program distribution had two main systems at that time. A syndication company that owned the rights to a show could sell it to a station for a certain number of airings in exchange for money. Or, they could offer the program, series, or programming package to a station on a barter basis, in which the station would hand back a certain number of commercial spots within the broadcast. The syndicator would then package the airtime from around the country to get a piece of national TV advertising dollars being spent.

Familiar to all viewers and relatively lucrative (as opposed to having unsold spots in low viewership time periods), is a fourth program option called "paid programming." In this model, a TV production company or packager/distributor buys the time periods from a station to air the show.

The broadcast networks and many program syndicators were asking local stations for more spots to offset ever-increasing production costs. This left the stations with less of an ability to generate cash, and the laws of supply and demand increased the value of the time periods we'd find acceptable for the *Health Matters* TV series. To get those time periods, stations started asking us to treat it like paid programming and to buy the time from them.

Annual program renewals became tougher. New markets were scarce, given the healthcare marketing paralysis. Pedro left the company. I was asked to focus on selling the local news inserts. Where I had once looked forward to diversifying my career, I was now back to selling exclusively to TV stations, and specifically to "news people," who in some respects didn't share a salesperson's focus on the holy dollar. And in retrospect, I didn't fully appreciate what made them tick.

Medstar now had a new management team in place, headed by a former TV station News Director and a hospital marketing guy. At lunch one day with Ron, the News Director now turned Sales Manager, I was urged to start looking for a new position. I asked if that was coming from him or from the owner. He said that "it was best for me and the company."

19

The next morning, I met with the owner who asked if Ron had spoken with me about my future with company. I said "yes," and asked if he was firing me. He quickly said, "No, we just want you to sell more. You can stay if you'll sell more." So, was I fired? Ron, the owner and I all knew that it was time for me to look elsewhere.

I cringe when I think back to part of my conversation with the owner that day. There I was, babbling about how I had been trying to get more deals closed, trying to develop new leads with health systems and the new target HMO's. I'd been trying to sell the news inserts. I was working long hours and going wherever there was a legitimate shot at making a sale.

He appreciated my efforts. Then, he offered two words which for me were a lifelong wake up call. He said, "Results matter."

The Trump Factor

WHNS-TV, FOX
Greenville, SC

T he less-than-gentle nudge to find employment elsewhere (OK, they canned my ass!) was a blow to my ego but had no disruption in my life's plan. Although the position at Medstar had enabled us to move out of New York, we always knew it would be temporary.

Our second winter in Allentown was greeted with much snow. In fact, I recall CBS News carried a season-long tally on the amount of snow falling in Boston versus the amount coming down in Eastern Pennsylvania. Both locales were experiencing tough winters.

At my house, we had our own special way to gauge the misery. If a snowfall was anything less than six inches, I'd shovel the driveway myself. Over six inches and we'd call a plow. That winter we called the plow seventeen times. We vowed not to spend another winter in Allentown.

My point in sharing an old weather report is its effect on sales. Although physically present and going through the daily motions, I had already "checked out." I think it's hard in sales to give it your best if you've already made up your mind to move on. Reps who find themselves actively investigating professional options with any determined pace or regularity may be fooling themselves if they claim they're just curious. Those same meetings and hours could be invested in revenue and commission-producing activities.

For a sales manager, learning that a rep is "out there looking" sets off an alarm that should not be ignored. It could explain a drop in the rep's productivity, or it might be a sign that the company is not meeting the needs that employees see as vital to their success. Was it just the rep's way of getting your attention? Is there a problem in the level of support, marketing, administrative assistance, product development or office management?

A key message in this chapter is that you have to like what you sell. No, your product or service doesn't have to define every aspect of your being. But you've got to feel good about it. Otherwise how can you realistically expect prospects to get excited?

At that time, I had a number of opportunities to explore sales positions with TV stations in many cities. I had worked with several hundred stations and developed some strong professional relationships with General Managers and Sales Managers.

While at Group W, the sale of our station image campaigns (i.e., "For Kids' Sake" and "Time to Care" among others) often had me and other regional managers for Group W training the local staff on how to sell and position the projects. Several contacts suggested that instead of looking for a traditional position as an account executive, I seek an opportunity allowing me to apply my expertise in generating non-traditional revenue.

Location. Location. Location. I had narrowed my relocation destination targets to a few cities – among them Charlotte, North Carolina and Atlanta, Georgia. I saw an ad in a trade publication seeking a Sales Marketing Manager which essentially described much of what I was desirous of doing. The job was with the Fox Television affiliate in Greenville, South Carolina, approximately midway between Charlotte and Atlanta.

Fox flew me down for an interview with Derek James, the General Manager. We seemed to click. I briefly met some others on the staff that day, including the General Sales Manager. I was informed I was a finalist. A few phone calls and exchanges later, I was offered the position and flown down to check out the area in greater detail with Ellen, my (seven months pregnant) wife.

Most memorable about our return trip home was landing in NY, getting in our car and having almost every radio station seemingly simulcast a bizarre police chase. Somewhere across the country on the freeways of Los Angeles, cops were in pursuit of a white Ford Bronco. We concluded that if Hall of Fame NFL star O.J. Simpson could be wanted for murdering his ex-wife and her friend, it wasn't so bizarre for us to move to Greenville, South Carolina.

People have a hard time believing me when I say that by 10:00 AM on my first day at WHNS-TV, I knew I had made a horrible career error. As Derek's assistant walked me around the station introducing me to the staff, people would yank me behind closed doors and say things like, "Really, why are you here?" "What are you gonna be doing because the GM and GSM never see eye to eye on anything?" "Who hired you, the GM or GSM? Did they actually discuss it together?"

Considering these comments came from the National Sales Manager, the Local Sales Manager and the stations' Operations Manager, I figured there were probably some more surprises ahead. At the end of the introductory walk-around, Derek walked me into Al Horton's office and advised I'd be reporting to him. Al, the General Sales Manager, showed as much cordiality and southern hospitality as most folks would show to a recurring hemorrhoid.

Lesson to reps everywhere: understand the chain of command. Understand the management style of your direct supervisor. Explore their willingness to be open to new ideas and be sure that you are on the same page when it comes to what is expected and required, as well as what is needed to achieve success.

Over the years, I've interviewed many salespeople looking for a new position because they were frustrated that their company could not provide an adequate product to be sold. I've met reps in this situation who sold a custom product and their sales levels outpaced capacity. I've also seen it with reps who sold a 'service' without the adequate personnel behind them to provide the required service in a timely fashion.

I've encountered this issue with numerous salespeople in the telecommunication world who went to work for companies because the companies were planning on building, wiring and "transmission towering" large areas. The companies then only partially completed their building plans, leaving unhappy customers angry at the reps.

I've encountered this issue with furniture salespeople who couldn't get product made in adequate supply because the manufacturers were moving production overseas and the reps got caught in the middle.

To sell special TV projects often meant packaging in promotional opportunities. At that time, there were no secondary channels or websites for cross promotion. The power of broadcast television wasn't supposed to rely exclusively on adjunct print components. A key challenge at WHNS at that time was that they were plain sold out – Greenville was (at that time) part of the 35th largest market in the country and only had four stations. TV spot inventory that could be packaged at lower rates to attract non-traditional advertisers was just not plentiful.

Lesson to reps everywhere: always carefully examine the production capacity, product sources, vendor relationships and availability of the products and services you'll be selling.

I once saw a list of "things that instill nervousness in typically calm people." The following were included as top nerve producers: having a baby, moving to a new city, buying a home and starting a new job. I was four for four! Ellen and our son had stayed behind in Pennsylvania. In her ninth month, the doctors didn't want her moving until after she gave birth.

The night before I was supposed to meet the lawyers to sign the papers buying our new house, I called Ellen and told her there was no way the job would work out. I asked, "Do you want me to quit and be unemployed up there or buy the house and be unemployed down here?"

Our goal was to move South. I was already there. The furniture was already half loaded on a moving van. I stayed at Fox and promised myself that for six months I would try to make it work. I knew that if I started looking, I couldn't give it a fair shot. On my six- month anniversary, I began looking and quickly found the position that would eventually allow my income to grow beyond the NY wages while living in a place we'd come to love.

One of the surprise television hits that year was *The Apprentice*, the reality program starring billionaire real estate tycoon Donald Trump (a guy who would later go into politics).

"The Donald" has written several fine business books, and it was his "presence" as well as his business acumen that led to his involvement with *The Apprentice*. Several friends highly recommended I watch the series, saying, "Like him or hate him, you'll love what he has to say about business."

For one reason or another it was late in the weekly elimination of the series when I got around to watching the show for my first time. Only a few contestants remained. Each sat dreading that now infamous line – "You're fired." I watched, fascinated, as Trump explained to the unfortunate target the reason they were fired.

His words ran something like, "There was no fire. There was no authentic enthusiasm. It was evident you were going through the motions and had no love for what you were doing. You've got to love what you commit to."

Now that is reality TV! That is also THE REALITY OF BS – BIG SALES, THAT IS!

Back then that Trump guy seemed to have a good head on his shoulders, and if the real estate gig didn't work out for him, I'd have been happy to consider him for a sales position. However, character matters!

A Simple Definition

McDonald's
Hamburger Joint, USA

I once interviewed a jerk. At least, that was the impression he left me with upon uttering these words: "I'm tired of working hard. I'm ready to do something easy, like sales." I'm not sure what he was comparing it to, but from our brief discussion and his resume, he wasn't spending his days digging ditches or performing manual labor.

All companies, whether they employ just a few reps or very large sales forces, have top reps as well as reps that just don't perform or deliver the same quality results. So, if sales is so simple, why don't we all just take the habits and actions of the top reps and have the entire sales force do those things?

When I left the world of television program sales, I entered the world of trade show marketing and exhibit sales, which is far more interesting, much more diverse, and allows for greater creativity. Shortly after I started with The Oliver Group, Nancy Gordon joined the company. During one of her client meetings, I overheard Nancy utilizing a line she'd heard me use a hundred times.

Now, Nancy was a brand-new college graduate. At the time, I had about fifteen years of sales experience. She stands about 5 foot nothing and I'm 6 foot 1. To hear the words come from Nancy, it was clear she was reciting a line. Whereas the same words coming from me, I like to believe, came across with conviction.

Nancy became a great salesperson and eventually went on to have sales and marketing jobs with large corporations. We can't expect salespeople to be robots, mimics or impersonators. Reps can identify positive traits of successful salespeople and personalize those attributes. But trying to come across as somebody else on an ongoing basis is a recipe for instilling distrust in your buyer, your support team or your employer.

A salesperson that was employed by our company (notice how I didn't say "worked for?") left us. When he was hired, we were all very excited over the prospect of his delivering big sales and lots of business. In fact, he had been a sales consultant for a nationwide business consulting firm. He could talk sales theory and list the needed steps to success – but for us, he never walked the talk. He never successfully took the steps.

So why didn't it work out for him? There is a difference between knowing what needs to be done and doing the work. It's one thing to say, "Sales means making lots of phone calls to set appointments." It's another thing to pick up the phone and make the calls. Or to dig deeply online to identify the right buyer. Or to knock on the doors. Or to greet the customers. Inherent in the definition of "successful sales" is that you've got to do the work.

Sometimes I refer to basic concepts as though they come from a universal Sales 101 or Marketing 101 college course. In other words, a foundation upon which further knowledge will reside. To define "sales" is challenging by virtue of the wide array of products, services, sellers, buyers, techniques and methodologies which the term incorporates. However, in one form or another, successful salespeople in all walks of life are adhering to the 101 concept of, "Sell benefits, not features."

Are you selling expensive software? How will its application enhance the life of the user? Unless you're talking to a fellow (said with affection) 'computer geek,' the minute you get into technical jargon you'll lose. But, tell the user, or the owner, how their life will be more productive and efficient, and you've got the potential for a sale. Nobody wants to buy software. They want to buy the benefits the software will deliver.

Do you sell expensive industrial machinery? Think of the difference between an opening which starts, "Hello, I'd like to speak with you about a major capital investment. It operates on 220v with conveyor function and electronic redundancy." Or, conversely, an opening which starts, "Hello, I'd like to talk with you about doubling your output, reducing labor costs and improving quality consistency."

I recently met with the marketing department of a well-known Sailboat manufacturer. They don't sell the height of their masts or the cubic footage of the heads – they sell lifestyle. "You, the dreamer who can afford it and the boating enthusiast who wants to move up. Picture yourself living the life, joining the ranks of the elite…"

Are you a clown with a big red nose, floppy feet and an all too familiar yellow outfit named Ronald McDonald? Do you sell hamburgers? People may have bought a zillion by now (I've stopped reading the signs that tell us how many they've sold) but how many go to McDonalds for the quality of their beef? Historically, the focus of McDonald's was on selling "convenience" and "familiarity." People know what to expect.

The software rep, the machinery salesperson and the sailboat company all understand that "sales" doesn't have to be complex. Here is my simple definition:

Sales is understanding what the prospect needs or wants, and positioning your product to meet that need or desire.

You Get One Chance To Make A First Impression

Time Warner Cable
Shreveport, LA

Anything and everything after the first impression is, quite simply, no longer the *first* impression. It's that first impression that sticks in a prospect's mind and serves as the barometer to which you'll forever be measured.

We're often more conscious of this fact in our personal lives than in the business world. If salespeople spent as much time on their opening lines as single people do in the pursuit of a date, their close ratios would be a lot higher. When the new in-laws are coming to your home for the first time, how careful are you to be sure everything is "just right?"

Although in most circumstances, buyers buy based on their own motivations, whom they buy from is a result of how they perceive your product, your company and your pricing. However, none of these factors come into play if they write off doing business with you because of – well, you!

Blowing the sale, or hearing that your prospect has purchased from a competitor, is neither fun nor something that will never happen to you. It will happen. It does happen. Nobody hits 1.000% in this league. Learning why a sale was lost can greatly help next time you come up to bat.

There are many sales that get lost because the rep was pushing a particular product. Perhaps inventory was backing up so there were special incentives (either to the customer or the rep) to push a product. You come out of the gate blabbering about an item that may not have any relevance to your prospect's needs. Forever, you'll be known as the rep who talked first and didn't listen.

There are many repeat sales that are lost because a rep didn't live up to the hype they created for the product, service or results. We had a lawn service that sold us on switching to their "all-natural approach" because "organic processes" would lead to healthier, weed free grass without all those "harmful chemicals" from which our kids would grow three heads. After one year of my formerly green grass turning brown and blotchy, they were out of there. The product and service didn't live up to expectations.

Sometimes you even lose when you win! Sometimes a client's expectations are set by their past experiences. UnderWraps International makes packaging equipment. Following a lengthy pursuit, I sold them what for our company was a relatively large project for the Pack Expo tradeshow.

They wanted to change their strategy of bringing huge equipment to the tradeshow and shift to a large-scale video presentation. As we went through several iterations of floorplans, they kept adding big machines back into the mix. Midway through the process the "decision maker" had a heart attack. I was then working with his number two while the boss recuperated.

Number Two voiced large concerns over price and continued to hold the prospect of their existing vendor still getting the job over my head. Ultimately, we packaged in extensive service, had a great design, and when the boss returned, we were awarded the job. Although the machinery was all still in the display, so was the video.

Without digressing further from the point at hand, let me just say McCormick Place in Chicago can be hectic even for simple trade shows. When an exhibitor has huge machinery in need of wiring, massive A/V screens and projection equipment, it can grow complex. Infamous for unions convoluting the process, at this show I once counted seven separate unions in our client's booth at the same time.

I flew out to Chicago for a few days of the set up. The Service Manager we employed at the show had been handling our clients in Chicago for years with generally high praise from clients. My biggest surprise at the show was arriving to find my major competitor working in the booth side by side with Number Two. Turns out my "competitor" was also a former UnderWraps employee.

My competition on the job had, in the past, not only provided the exhibits and graphics but also coordinated the client's equipment installation with the union millwrights. The client brought him out to the show to perform that service even though we were providing the exhibit.

After the show it took a while to get all of the costs reconciled. There are some fees that get billed directly from a tradeshows' general contractor to the exhibitor and are not billed through the exhibit provider. The client was incredulous that we had not included one of these fees in our charges to him. Was it an oversight?

No. We never pre-billed something that was not in our control and would only cost the client more if we had to mark it up. However, his past experience was that it was pre-billed.

So why include this saga in a chapter on "first impressions?"

Because I have little expectation we'll ever do business with the client again. Did we do anything wrong? Incomplete? Underhanded? Was there anything promised that was not delivered? No. However, in their minds, the client's first experience with us was less than ideal. Why would anyone want to risk that again?

Sometimes we blow a sale based on the impression we make before we open our mouths. Is the vehicle you're driving working for you or against you? In some professions it may be a plus to drive the shiny new Mercedes. In others, it may send a message that your prices are too high. In some professions pulling up in a Kia or Ford Escort might send a message that you are frugal, and therefore affordable. To some buyers you might be seen as unsuccessful and in need.

Whether driving a brand-new Tesla or a twenty-year-old Kia, do your best to keep it clean. You never know when a prospect is looking out the window to see who drives up.

Our clothing, too, may create an impression in the buyer's mind. Ditto for hair, make-up, jewelry and the briefcase we carry. Before we open our mouths, buyers are already characterizing us. It's simply human nature to create an opinion based on observation. We recently decided not to hire a relatively strong candidate for a sales position based solely on their appearance.

"Appearance" is not limited to your physical attributes. There is an intangible that we call "presence" which is derived from someone's manner and demeanor. It starts with the observable appearance and continues through to the hand shake, the opening lines, the posture and other non-verbal traits in addition to what is said.

Sincerity versus being slick. Pleasant and jovial versus boisterous and cantankerous. These are part of presence. These make up a part of the first impression. These determine if someone will buy your product or service.

Retailers understand the importance of "environment." Compare a Whole Foods market to an off-price discount market. Cleanliness and clutter affect a buyer's impression of the product or its relative value.

Many businesses recognize the importance of first impressions. In general, the lobby of an ad agency will be funkier than the lobby of a doctor's office or law firm. In any of these cases, the company may recognize the value of a strong receptionist. In fact, some companies have named that position "Director of First Impressions." The first thing a prospect hears is what starts the process of how they perceive your company.

I now live in the South. Despite what some of my Northern friends think, not everyone is met by the greeting of "Howdy!" Wherever you live, think of how you perceive people differently if they greet you with, "How ya doin'?" "Hey!" "Wassup?" or "Good afternoon." What can you say to be cordial, memorable and impactful?

Another 'first impression' area that all reps need to re-examine is their correspondence and literature. "Spellcheck" on computers has exacerbated an already declining ability to properly spell words in the English language. I'm relatively certain that trend holds true in many other cultures and languages throughout the world.

I cringe when I receive solicitations that have misspellings. I throw out resumes and cover letters. If a rep can't create a good first impression when they are selling themselves, why would an employer expect them to do any better selling their products?

In the late '80's the cable television business was on the bottom of everyone's list when it came to customer service. I was working for Group W selling a TV Station Community Image campaign called "Time To Care." One of my assigned markets was Shreveport, Louisiana. None of the four local broadcasters were interested in the project.

About that time, I had started some discussions with cable systems (multiple system operators) about developing projects for use on their system's local access channels. With my thoughts turning to expanding our customer base, I tried a new approach to selling my product and set an appointment with the manager of the local cable company in Shreveport.

He had been brought in because of significant declines in subscriber retention, problems with the City Council and a general public relations problem in how Time Warner was perceived by its prospects in Shreveport. The manager shared that their possible interest in our product was centered on the need to repair their image. The cable operator was seen as unprofessional, sloppy in their work, overpriced and an arrogant monopoly.

This manager's family had just joined him in their new town the previous week. The day before our meeting they had moved into their new home. Now, on the second day in their new house, his local cable installers were coming to hook up his family.

I don't know if he paid the same monthly bill as all subscribers in town, or if cable was included in his employment contract. However, assuming for a moment his family was like any other, the cable system would have the presumption of making a monthly sale to him for as long as they lived in the house.

That morning his wife answered the door to greet the installers. One (exceptionally heavy, pants not fully covering the crack in his butt when he bends type) installation person was wearing a black T-shirt. It read, "We have *cum* for your daughters."

Is it any wonder the image of the system was in need of repair?

Note to reps everywhere: zealously create and guard the first impression you and your company create. You will always be playing catch up if you blow it!

The Dirty Little Secret
To Sales Success

Gorgeous, Fresh off the Manufacturing Line
BMW 740

W e'll start this chapter back in fourth grade. Some of the most important things you need to know about sales were taught back then. Whether you're 25 or 52 years of age, somewhere back in elementary school, even back to Nursery School, "mathematics" was something you had to learn.

Think of all the times you use math in the course of your business day. We provide pricing for our prospects and clients. We deal with quantities of items ordered. We work with budgets. We count cash or invoices. And, if you're good, you review your commission percentages!

There is a saying in business that goes, "Sales cures all ills." But if the sales are not profitable or do not yield acceptable margins, then more sales may not be the answer to your company's challenge. Perhaps then, the answer is more revenue per sale.

The concept of "more" is generally a good one when it comes to sales. However, when I consult with companies going to tradeshows, I am careful to point out that their goal isn't necessarily to meet with "as many" people as possible, but as many "qualified prospects" as possible.

This admonition goes to all salespeople, too. If "more" is good, "more who are more qualified to buy from you" is better!

Back now to math class. Let's say on average you close business with 20% of the prospects you encounter. If that's the case, during the course of a week would you rather meet with ten prospects and make two sales, or fifteen prospects and make three sales? More is better.

Still in math class. Let's say on average you make five sales per week. Remember, we're being very generic and simple here since some of you sell million-dollar items and some of you sell products or services with price points measured in pennies. Would you rather that your five sales had a price point of $100 per sale, or $150 per sale? More is better.

If you know that on average you can get about five new appointments for every 100 emails you blast out or calls you attempt, are you better sticking to 100, or making it 200? More is better.

What if you sell a limited commodity? In my television days, broadcasters were highly regulated as to the amount of airtime or commercial spots they could sell in any given hour during parts of the day. They could "sell out" if they just kept selling more?

The same concept would hold true for a hotel as they only have a finite number of rooms. This challenge of "capacity control" would also apply to airline seats. Keep selling more and there is nothing left to sell.

While some would consider this a good problem to have, the answer for these industries is to get more money for the same item as scarcity increases. It is simple supply and demand. Understand the numbers – sales is a numbers game.

During my short tenure with Fox Television in Greenville, a local business development that would change the face, accent and business makeup of South Carolina for decades to come came to fruition. BMW broke ground in Greer, South Carolina on its first manufacturing plant outside of Europe.

In the twenty-five years since the first earth was moved to build its factory, BMW has grown to the point of assembling approximately 1,900 vehicles on a daily basis. Direct employment is about 8,800 relatively high paying jobs and well over 100 new manufacturing companies have been drawn to our area largely to service BMW.

Sean Calais, now a highly prominent government figure, was at this time the Communications Manager for BMW. I represented a local television station ranked fourth in a four-station market, which primarily ran kids programming, re-runs and bad movies. Without any particular roadmap to follow as to how I was supposed to develop business with the 8,000 pound upscale manufacturing gorilla in town, I picked up the phone and called him.

Two weeks later, Sean picked me up at the station and we went to lunch. Many employees at BMW have the option of participating in a company subsidized vehicle lease program. Senior executives were either given cars or had the opportunity to lease the high-end vehicles. I believe Sean's car was fresh off the production line that week.

On the drive to the restaurant we exchanged pleasantries and backgrounds. Me, being the foreigner, and he, the local boy from Columbia, SC, Sean shared some advice about doing business in the South. He told the story of two bulls.

A Northern bull and a Southern bull amble to the crest of hill and look down upon a valley filled with cows. The Northern bull says to his southern bovine friend, "I'm gonna run down into that valley and fast as I can make love to one of those cows." The Southern bull responds, "I'm gonna walk down, take my time and make love to all the cows!" More is better.

The dirty little secret to sales success is volume.

The M.A.N. Qualifier

Riverfront Hotel
St. Paul, MN

No ladies, "The M.A.N. Qualifier" is nothing you'll find in the pages of *Cosmo*. And no, gents, it isn't something you'll reference in your favorite sporting magazine to see if you measure up. "M.A.N." is an easy-to-recall acronym and "qualifying" is among the greatest gifts you, as a salesperson, can give to yourself.

I first encountered "The M.A.N. Qualifier" at a Worldwide Expo put on by Skyline Exhibits in Minnesota several years back. I was in a hotel bouncing between scheduled sessions when I ran into a friend from another city and we decided to get a cup of coffee and catch up. By the time I got to the appointed seminar room, the chairs were full and I made my way around the back of the room, slithering behind curtains to avoid accentuating my late arrival.

Written on an easel awaiting its turn to be revealed by the presenter was the word "MAN." John Lomen, who would go on to be Skyline's full-time trainer, was presenting the session and defined the term as follows:

"M" is for money. Unless the prospective client has the money or can get it in the future, there is not going to be a sale! They may love your product and recognize its benefits, but if they can't pay you then don't waste your time.

"A" is for authority. Everyone should be familiar with the goal of dealing with a decision maker and not a gatekeeper. Until you are dealing with someone who can authorize the purchase, while you may be getting closer to a sale, you're still nowhere.

"N" is for need. In business-to-business sales there are not too many things purchased unless the client perceives there to be a need. In selling to consumers, the word "need" may be substituted by "desire." I might buy a new pair of shoes because I like them even if I don't need them, but the likelihood of a company making a major capital purchase purely based on "liking something" is small.

A review of the "M.A.N." qualifiers can benefit salespeople in several ways. First, it's a great litmus test to ensure you are investing your time in pursuit of a project that has a good chance of closing. Second, along with several other techniques discussed elsewhere in this book, "M.A.N." should become part of your "post mortem" exercises when you lose a sale.

Certainly, 20/20 hindsight can be a wonderful teacher. Go back to an opportunity that you felt should have closed but didn't. What about the first step in "M.A.N." – "money" – could you have missed?

Did you forget to inquire about the client's fiscal year or budget cycle? Did you fail to ascertain their purchasing logistics? Was it as simple as you being blindsided by an enthusiastic prospect who had champagne dreams but only a beer budget?

What did you miss regarding the second step, "authority?" Were you working with a "direct contact" whose purchasing authority was capped and the ability to buy something at your price point involved others who were not part of your presentations? Was there a hidden "final decision maker" which might be a board or an individual? Were you trying to "sell in" at the executive level when the users of your product (decision influencers) had never voiced their preference?

Look at a common consumer purchase such as a car. Many car salesmen have regrettably invested time with one spouse, test driving and custom designing the prospect's dream vehicle, when the other spouse has already laid down the law that the new car will be "Auto X."

What did you miss regarding the final step, "need?" Did it fail to occur to you, in the heat of the sales battle, that you were just selling them what they already had, and therefore there was no need to switch to your product? Did you fail to uncover what about their current vendor needed to be improved upon? Did you concentrate on the features of your product instead of demonstrating how the customer would benefit *because* those features fulfilled a need their business was experiencing?

Remember "money," "authority," and "need." Spend your time with prospects who are "the M.A.N."

Why I Passed On The Passat And Spent More On A Lexus

Muddy Ditch
Greer, SC

I n terms of sales, this lesson really begins at the Tong Hoy Chinese restaurant in Larchmont, NY. Although technically, I believe in their later years they moved across the road which would have put them in Mamaroneck. Either way, sadly it's too late to enjoy their soup, eggrolls and spareribs. Tong Hoy is no longer with us.

My children and I went up to New York for a family visit. Ellen had remained in South Carolina for the weekend. We had found good airfares flying in and out of the Asheville airport about sixty miles away. Whatever the cost savings was, it justified the extra drive since the Greenville airport was only five minutes from our house.

Greenville is a great restaurant town for a city its size, but until very recently its Chinese food left a lot to be desired (show me a New Yorker who won't criticize other cities' pizza and Chinese food and I'll tell you they probably live in Jersey). We loaded up at Tong Hoy on about $100 worth of food and had it packed to travel. We carried that food through LaGuardia and our connecting airport, then out to our car through a torrential rainstorm in the North Carolina mountains.

It was very late on a Sunday night. The kids were young and fairly quickly fell asleep in the back of the Saab as I drove home. Leaving the interstate

41

south of Hendersonville I came down the mountain on Route 25 then cut over on a winding two-lane road. Like so many areas of our city, about eight miles from our house there was a lot of construction and the two-lane ran through it.

Now, on the far side of midnight, dark, wet and tired, I was navigating through a temporary road detour due to the construction. Whether it was wind or kids being evil, someone or something had turned the detour sign to point in the wrong direction. Following this path, the Saab left pavement and entered gravel. We left gravel and found dirt. I followed the dirt road tracks another forty yards and was now in a giant mud puddle made worse by the minute from the rain. The tires spun. I cursed.

For the next thirty minutes I gently tried rocking the car between drive and reverse to get out of the rut. But it was more like a swamp. In a situation such as this, man's natural instinct to gun the engine and let shear power pull you out doesn't work. I know, I tried.

Eyeing a construction dumpster up the embankment I climbed out, waddled through the mud and retrieved huge chunks of thick cardboard materials that I hoped would give the tires traction. Wrong again. Time for help. It wasn't as though we were in the middle of nowhere. A gas station was (back on paved earth) only about 200 yards away.

The sleeping angels were now half-awake in the backseat. Kara, my daughter, was about four. She was swathed in her ever-present pink blanket ("Bankie"). Craig, my eight-year-old son, was being the brave man, hugging both his sister and "George," the stuffed monkey who had been with him since birth.

I told the kids to just wait in the car while I ran over to the gas station. Now approaching 1:00 AM on a dark, rainy night, a sweaty, panting, mud-covered lunatic aroused the attendant from her sleep, screaming about "kids stuck in a car in a mud swamp off the road." It was then that I cursed the gods of economic evolution who turned most gas stations into convenience stores instead of automotive repair shops that had tow trucks! This was a job for Triple A!

Another thirty-five minutes on the phone with AAA trying to find a tow truck working in the Greer area at 1:30 AM on a Sunday night/Monday morning proved fruitless. Somewhere along the line, my paternal instinct got the better of my patience. I gave up on help from the outside world and returned to the car just in time to find my frightened kids had removed their shoes, rolled up their pants and were about to make a break for the gas station. Time for a superhero. We called Mommy.

I asked Ellen to at least come and pick the kids up and we'd figure out the car later on. Figuring she needed a little time to fully wake up, get dressed, and drive 10 minutes or so to our location, I had some time to try to still drive out of the predicament. This final attempt started as the others had ended, with no movement, lots of tire-spinning and engine racing. Lots and lots of engine racing. Then, something caught, and we slid a bit.

The slide turned into a series of 360's and on one turn we caught some dirt dry enough to propel us forward. With a bit of traction, I was now gunning it so as not to lose the momentum. We were edging out of the mud pit! The kids and monkey cheered. Bankie waved. We left mud and found dirt. I followed dirt to gravel. I couldn't tell if I was sweating from adrenaline or the heat of the moment. Gravel turned back into pavement. We were out. We were cheering. We were exasperated and we were hot.

I drove up the road a bit, simply to get some distance between us and the pit of doom. Then I pulled over to catch my breath and check all was OK in the back seat. The cell phone rang. It was Ellen searching for us. Within seconds of stopping the car it filled with smoke. Where there's smoke, there's fire. I screamed into the phone, "The car's on fire!" and jumped out, grabbing a kid under each arm and running behind a building for safety.

The only light was the flames coming from the front of the Saab. My daughter, through her tears, had one word for me, "Bankie!" This led to my son hysterically realizing George was trapped in the flaming vehicle. In what I consider to be the stupidest thing I've ever done, I ran back to the inferno of an auto and rescued the blanket and monkey. Running back to the safety of the building, behind me, I heard a loud explosion!

It was in this manner that my "buyers need" for a new car was created.

As we huddled in the rain watching the car burn, it seemed help had found us. Through the downpour, lights of a fire engine could be seen. The emergency vehicle was a hybrid fire truck and ambulance. I rushed to greet our saviors to be met by two EMTs who didn't emerge from their truck.

I was thankful they were there and asked who had called them. "Nobody called us, mister, we've got a guy having a heart attack in the back of the truck. Hey, is that your car on fire over there?" They agreed to call our problem in to the dispatcher and pulled away with their patient.

At that same moment Ellen pulled up to find me standing in the road, mud covered, looking distraught as an ambulance pulls away. To this day I regret the moment of panic she must have experienced until she saw our kids run out from behind the building.

After the firemen arrived and put out the flames, they continued to spray down the car's exterior. Two firemen were sweeping pieces of Saab off the road and I meekly asked, "Do you think it can be fixed?" They confirmed my buyers need.

Then, the cruelest blow of all. Just shy of 3:00 AM they were able to pry open the trunk so we could get personal effects out. The Chinese food from New York was still intact but I was urged not to salvage it. Something about flame spray chemicals, noxious gases and MSG not properly mixing.

Within a few days we began our search for a new car. I was smitten with the VW Passat. In fact, most things we looked at couldn't penetrate my single-minded desire to get that car. Ellen was all for it and having decided on the Passat we went to Victor Black Volkswagen on Greenville's Auto Mile. That's when we fell victim to the attack of the car salesman.

His abrasive demeanor and non-stop talking was a turn-off. His failure to recognize an easy sale was a crime. Turning the pricing discussion into a game was his death knell. Despite the decision being made, the money in hand and the need clearly present, this sales rep lost a $28,000 sale because of his personality. His employer lost the sale (and surely countless others) because of poor training.

Not only didn't they recognize our "buying signals," but frankly, the man was an irritant. Buyers frequently relate products back to their buying experience. There was no way I wanted to think about that jerk every time I got into my car.

Just up the road from the VW place was the Lexus dealer. Knowing we couldn't afford or wouldn't spend the money on a Lexus, we stopped in just for a break from the real shopping. Melanie, the saleswoman at Lexus, recognized a tired family frustrated in their search for a product they needed.

She asked some questions. She offered cold drinks and comfortable couches. She learned about who would drive it and how the car would be utilized. There was no pressure. But she was clearly guiding her prospects on a self-actualization process that led from dreaming of owning a Lexus to driving a Lexus.

The showrooms and service areas at many luxury car dealerships are nicer and more pleasing than many other car places. They understand that the buying decision is affected by the selling process and the selling process is affected by the environment. They understand it is far more productive to help a consumer buy than to pressure sell to them.

Companies everywhere could enhance their efficiency by closely studying the effects of their rep's personality and approach as well as the environment created by their selling process. One of the key elements to BS is if they don't like you, they won't buy from you.

The Great Motivators

As a sales professional, you have an obligation, a need, and a mandate to understand what it is that motivates your customers. Once you stop to think about it, you'll discover that you'll sell more by positioning your product or service in a manner that addresses the prospect's motivation.

Seems simple. But it's not.

Let's look at the manufacturing company that has always bought parts from a particular vendor. Forty years earlier, the first sale between the companies was consummated. It was easy because the two owners were friends. Over the years, both companies have changed hands several times, but the vendor-customer relationship has remained intact. Why?

Is it because the product is an intrinsic part of the manufacturer's production process? Maybe.

Is it because the purchasing agent at the manufacturer is lazy and doesn't want to "work" to shop for alternative vendors? Maybe.

Is it because the product supplier makes an exceptional product that has always been reliable? Maybe.

Is it because the longevity of the relationship is such that potential rivals for the parts business have never pursued the account? Maybe.

Is it because the purchasing agent is tired of arguing with the production department, or is afraid to make a mistake? Maybe.

Is it because even though many competitors have been buying less costly parts, using this part makes this manufacturer unique and gives them the ability to make quality claims when selling their product? Maybe.

What motivates your buyers? What keeps your prospects from becoming customers? Can you pinpoint *the real reason* you made your five biggest sales?

Buying decisions made by companies are actually made by people. Always remember that there is a person behind the "prospect" and that people are funny animals. Sometimes, their motivations are pure and in the best interest of the company. Other times, they may make a decision because it is easier or carries the least likelihood of backfiring.

The reasons that consumers and businesspeople buy are as varied as the world around us. However, there are two broad categories of buyer motivation that I refer to as the "Great Motivators." They are FEAR and GREED. These categories can be applied to most types of sales.

Let's examine two types of purchasing decisions. Something as simple as whether to buy a new blouse at a woman's clothing store can be dissected in the same manner as a complex worldwide services contract for security and plant maintenance.

The woman deciding to buy the blouse at the mall may 'fear' not looking as good as others at the party she'll be attending. She may 'fear' that all the clothing in her closet is old and dated, and that is not how she wants to be perceived. She may 'fear' being seen in something previously worn. She may 'fear' that her significant other is tired of seeing her in "the same old thing."

The salesperson at the clothing store should seek to uncover the customer's motivation. Its no longer about "how can I help you," but "how can I help you look good to your date, look better than the younger woman, remain chic, etc..."

On the other hand, perhaps the self-confident blouse shopper is motivated more by 'greed.' She may want to look "the best" at the party. She may want to impress a particular person or be the first to wear a hot designer outfit. In these cases, the salesperson in the clothing store can play to the 'greed.' "You'll be the first one in town wearing *hotsy-totsy*." "Not only will this one guy want you, but every man in the room will have his eyes on you."

Fear and greed serve as the basis for most business purchases, too. Let's look at our second example of a large industrial maintenance and security firm going after the worldwide contract for a company with numerous locations throughout the globe.

The buyer has 'fears' over the security of its personnel, its production capabilities, and the safety of its inventories, distribution networks, and communications systems. It has hundreds of millions invested in physical structures. And any major breakdown in its production capabilities may shut down its organization around the world, costing millions in revenue daily.

The security and maintenance vendor can play to those concerns, demonstrating how they are equipped to avoid the exact types of incidents their worldwide prospect fears. They can illustrate the ways they've helped companies maintain production through periodic maintenance and/or a production redundancy plan. They can point to satellite-fed worldwide security monitoring that reinforces the onsite personnel's efforts.

In other words, they can paint the worst scenarios to "accentuate the pain," and then position their services to aid the prospect in avoiding those fears.

But much like the simple sale of the blouse, this complex, international, multi-point contract can also be pursued on the basis of greed.

Would this company not want to offer its personnel *the best* security available to the private sector? Just think of the benefits the company would reap if it could tell its clients that production readiness was guaranteed through both periodic maintenance coordinated the world over, as well as an automatic instant production redundancy plan in the event of a temporary shutdown?

The same service is being positioned in a different manner: when fear is the motivation, you seek out and paint a negative that your prospect wants to avoid. When greed is the variable at hand, you dangle and entice with positives. These are the two "great motivators" which form the foundation of most decision making. It is your job to figure how they apply to your situation.

A major difference in selling to consumers versus selling to businesses is that consumer motivation has a greater tendency to be based on "desire" versus "need." I *might* decide to buy a new pair of shoes today, but I *know* I'm not going to go to work barefoot. When selling to consumers, there often isn't the same "need" as there is in the business that will purchase or lease a new copy machine because theirs broke last week.

Indeed, while I may want or desire a pair of shoes I see in a store, the business with the broken copier *needs* a new machine. The copier salesperson should recognize that the business doesn't want to buy his product – they just need the end result his product provides. And the shoe salesman should recognize that I don't need to buy the shoes, I just want them.

When I was in college, several friends and I took a road trip from Syracuse, NY down to Florida. Anyone who has driven to South Florida understands the letdown that sets in a few hours after you enter the state and you're still not there yet. Our crew decided liquid therapy was in order, and well after midnight found a biker bar on the beach in Daytona that was still open.

We parked the car on the beach, which is legal, although I think high tide plays a part in that decision. Emerging several hours later, we got back in the car. The car's owner was in the driver's seat. He gunned the engine and started heading south, driving along the hard-packed sand on the beach.

I can't say what demon entered my friend's head, but all of a sudden he screamed, "What the hell!" He veered left, driving head-first into the

Atlantic Ocean. (Note to readers everywhere: while Subaru wagons are nice cars, they are not seaworthy.) By the way, did you know the ocean has an undertow strong enough to suck a car further out to sea?

It may not surprise you that even at 4:00 AM during Christmas break, Daytona Beach could draw a crowd. Crowds, of course, draw the police, and that wasn't entirely bad as we needed them to radio for a tow truck. Apparently, there was a fee to be negotiated and my friend didn't like the terms or the level of service the old guy in the tow truck was offering.

By the minute, the Subaru was getting deeper. Failing to conclude the sale, the old tow truck driver got in his truck and patiently waited while we enlisted the help of other drunken college kids and tried to push the car back up to shore. Of course, Mother Nature and the tow truck driver knew this was impossible.

When we gave in and agreed to his offer, the price doubled. At that point, he fully understood we were motivated by a true *need*.

The more you know about your prospect's situation, the greater your chance of concluding big sales.

Why?

WSMV-TV
Nashville, TN

Whether you actually ask it, or simply seek to understand "why" someone is considering a purchase, that little question is an important piece in your quest for big sales.

Understanding buyer motivation is as essential to successfully concluding deals as is the product itself.

"Why?" can lead the sales representative down the correct path. It can help you solve a problem the prospect is experiencing. It can provide you with information that sets the tone for negotiation. After all, if a customer *wants* something, they may very well be willing to walk away if your price or some other factor is not to their liking. However, if the prospect *needs* something, your position as the vendor is strengthened.

"Why" helps a rep recommend the proper solution. The financial planner selling investments has many to offer a customer. Knowing what the goals are is essential to selecting the correct investment vehicle. And speaking of "vehicles," the car salesman who learns about a "soccer mom's" carpool habits when asking why she needs the extra seating that is shooting her budget will likely look for another area to shave the price.

In my company, we ask a lot of "why" questions. In addition to helping us learn about client needs, we can use "why" as a sales tool. For example, if a client expresses a need for a podium, we ask, "Why?" If their answer is that they need a place for literature, we can offer an alternative at a fraction of the cost.

By learning their need had nothing to do with the benefits and features of a podium (storage, a place to write, a need to lean on something, or a shelf for product, A/V or computers), we can offer a literature shelf as an alternative solution. What we are really offering is a way for the client to save money and more efficiently use the space in their exhibit booth.

As a sales tool, what we've done is position ourselves as an ally to the client. No longer are we perceived as the "greedy salespeople" trying to take their money – in fact, we've suggested ways to save money. The intent is to legitimately earn their trust. Without that initial trust, little of value will be shared during "discovery." And the chances of their ultimately selecting us as a vendor are slim.

It's not very different in most buyer-seller relationships. The purchaser will generally be less suspicious of a salesperson who positions a viable option, then offers a less costly alternative that is equal or superior in quality.

Asking "why" on the front side of a sales relationship should not preclude you from asking "what else" on the back side. It's an opportunity to gain referrals, to learn about other areas of the company you may be able to sell to, or to learn about future needs of the same client.

By focusing on the thing that is motivating them to purchase in the first place, and offering an effective solution, it is then that you earn the right to *effectively* ask for more of their business. Asking prematurely can set the wrong tone for the relationship.

As a Marketing Consultant, one of the things I repeatedly work on with clients is getting them to realize nobody cares about what is being sold. Clients care about how what they buy will affect them. Put simply, nobody cares about your stuff – they only care about how your stuff will make them richer, faster, better looking, more efficient, less stressed.

The concept is a simple Marketing 101 theorem that states: sell benefits, not features. Or, as my dad used to say, "Sell the sizzle, not the steak." I don't want to buy a stereo system, but I do want music in my home. I don't want to buy a copy machine, but I need to print out information. I may not care about the engineering jargon in the widget you want to sell me, but it damn well better be the part I need to keep the rest of my machinery running.

As a sales rep, your ability to combine the power of "why" with an understanding of selling benefits means you'll get ahead fast. Reps that don't get it struggle for years in mediocrity. Some reps understand one concept, but not the other.

I know a rep that is excellent about getting to the core of a client's intent. But the rep shoots himself in the foot repeatedly by taking that powerful information shared by the prospect and completely disregarding it. He insists on spewing out every bit of minutiae and detail until prospects go screaming for another source to buy from.

I also know reps who are good at staying focused on the benefits and never elongate a process with needless details. The problem is that by merely rattling off a generic list of benefit statements, they fail to make the product relevant to any one particular buyer. Without first discovering what they need, why they need it, and what is motivating the inquiry, it's hard to pick which of the product's benefits should be highlighted.

Midway in this chapter, I want to acknowledge a whole class of sales that is perhaps simpler, but certainly no less competitive. Some products are bought because they look good and the price is right – if you're lucky enough to sell something that isn't complex, don't ruin a good thing by making the sales process complicated!

Understanding the dynamics involved in a sales process means recognizing the buyer motivation on levels both personal (the individuals involved) and corporate (the interaction of people and the collective need motivating them). Cultures, budgets, egos, policies and procedures are just a few of the things that can get in the way of a sale being made.

In an earlier chapter of this book, we discussed fear and greed, as well as need and desire. Another way to look at your business is to determine if people are buying your services and products as a defensive move or an offensive move.

An example of a defensive purchase is the retailer that buys a rep's products because they can get exclusivity and prevent a promising product from attracting shoppers to a competitor's store. Another example is the corporation that purchases a sponsorship of an event not because they want to be associated with it or gain from its exposure, but because they do not want their competitor gaining from exposure or association.

For many years, Skyline Exhibits purchased the advertising rights on the back cover of Exhibitor Magazine. It was great to keep any competitors from gaining the perceived high-exposure benefit of the prominent placement. Tracking leads and analyzing market research eventually showed our marketing team the ROI wasn't worth the continued investment. The publishers and ad salesman lost the ability to sell us using a defensive strategy since we no longer cared if anyone else bought the space. We knew buying it was not helping us.

They were also stymied by not being able to use an offensive motivation pitch. Appealing to a buyer's need for a strong offense means your product will give them an advantage or enable them to become a leader. Our research showed (and a study in their magazine later confirmed) we were already a leader, with a number of clear advantages over our target market.

Offensive motivational positioning of a product is used far more often than defensive positioning. One appeals to business people's natural tendency to be optimists. The other is reminding them of the need to be on their guard, cautious, and mindful of the competition.

As a rep, understanding which card to play and in what manner to position your product to a buyer calls for a strategy. Remind yourself of your company's strategies – even if you are a company of one.

When you combine the power of "why" with a determination of whether to take an offensive or defensive approach, you open up multiple avenues to pitch the same product. This works best when you offer something in limited supply and high demand.

I had appointments set at the three main television network affiliates in Nashville, TN. All three meetings were on the same day, which happened to be a Friday in the summertime. The package of programming I was pitching could only be sold to one station. I went to see the top station in the market last. They were an incumbent customer but had previously negotiated lower-than-market rates for the program package.

The first station I called on that day had some interest, but I didn't foresee them making a legitimate offer. Luckily, my second station appointment was both interested and serious. They were in a major expansion mode and felt our package would help their promotions, programming, news and community relations. They gave me a firm offer but also understood I had an obligation to our incumbent to give them a chance to better the offer.

By understanding "why" this station was interested, I was able to best position the product. I shifted the focus of my pitch from one highlighting the sales and revenue potential to one that addressed their on-air and outreach needs. It was giving them a tool to help their "offense."

When I arrived in mid-afternoon at my last meeting with the incumbent, I was part of an agenda that had apparently started hours earlier and included a "liquid lunch" for some of the managers. They were boisterous, rude, arrogant, and absolutely convinced that all they had to do was throw out a lowball offer and I'd sell them the package.

In just a few short minutes I realized they didn't care about using the programming package to its fullest extent (they had never applied it properly in the past) and that unless I did something dramatic, there was not a serious offer forthcoming. I wasn't free to divulge any specifics of the offer from the other station, but in this case, knowledge was power.

In a boardroom crowded with about a dozen people, right after someone's "let's give the sales rep some crap" Friday afternoon joke, I abruptly stood up and announced I was leaving. For the first time, I had their attention.

Their General Sales Manager said, "You can't go, we haven't made you an offer yet." I replied, "Why should I waste my time with a presentation when all it will do is elicit a lowball offer? I already have an extremely appealing offer from your competition along with a plan to make best use of the project." I continued, "If you don't want them eating your lunch, get serious and here is what it will cost you…"

I closed my briefcase and left the room. In the twenty-minute drive to the airport, my secretary told me they had called my office twice. Appealing to their "offense" made no sense, because they didn't perceive the need to use the project offensively. But understanding that their motivation lay in not wanting a competitor to have the chance at success allowed me to successfully defensively position the project.

Ultimately who won? Well, after the bidding war that raised the market rate for the project, I did!

Fill 'Er Up!

The Oliver Group
Greensboro, NC

Before I was promoted (the day I left the fun behind), I reported to a manager who I ultimately replaced. He and the owner of the company parted ways largely over a discrepancy over how to treat people. She was a believer in respect, support and leadership. He wasn't.

However, he did have some excellent insights. He used to preach, "Not all business is good business!" We all have accounts that zap our time, energy and spirit and we'd be better off without them.

We can learn from everyone around us, good or bad. While I disagree with the old manager's tactics, I very much appreciated his understanding of and emphasis on the need to keep your sales pipeline full.

At monthly sales meetings he would select a rep and seat them in the center of a circle surrounded by the rest of the salespeople and sometimes the support staff, too. Reps had to lug their D.E.I. boards to the meeting. The D.E.I. Management Group was a sales training company run by Steve Schiffman. A key product of theirs was the prospect management tool.

Long before sales reps managed their databases, they had to manage the flow of prospects and accounts. Before we computerized, we used a system our manager had learned about at a seminar put on by Schiffman. Every time you had a new piece of business, you'd take an index card and enter the company name, your contact's name and phone number, a word or two to describe the product they were interested in, and the potential value of the business.

The cards were then put on a board with four vertical columns. Each column represented a different and progressive stage in the sales process. The far-left column was for new items and future appointments. In the adjacent column the project was in development, where either the rep was working on it or awaiting additional client input. Column three came to mean the prospect was in decision mode. And column number four was for 'index cards' representing business you felt would become a sale within the next thirty days.

Our D.E.I. boards were about two feet wide by four feet tall. We created the boards by wrapping felt around extra thick cardboard. The index cards were Velcroed on. The goal was to get as many cards on the board as possible (more potential business) and to keep them moving across the board (or moving through your sales pipeline). A rep could look at their board and know what had a 90% chance of closing in the next thirty days. Or, they could look at their board and know that next month meant eating cat food instead of steak.

The old manager would have the rep that was seated in the center of the circle explain their pipeline. It was high-pressure, and his approach of berating and embarrassing overshadowed the good that he likely intended to come out of it.

Legitimately, reps were expected to know what business each prospect was in. Reps were expected to know the next step and have a timetable and plan for each account. Reps were expected to know the competitive situation they faced on any particular piece of business. Reps were expected to know the level of decision-making authority their contacts had. And Reps were expected to maintain a full pipeline that would ensure adequate sales versus their quotas.

Today, when most pipeline visualizations are generated by reports, charts or funnels created by a rep's database, all of these are still good solid management expectations.

You, the salesperson, as the key manager of your business, should at least have these same goals for yourself. And if you want to beat yourself up for not doing what is expected, that's fine. Just be leery if you ever find yourself working for someone who gets off more on the beating up than on the sales success!

When I joined the company, I made the decision that my goal was to keep my board filled. It was easier and quicker to measure my board than to have my primary goal be to sell a certain amount. Measuring the pipeline was an instant snapshot of activity. If the activity is there and you're right for the job, the sales will come. Not everyone is right for the job. Not everyone is capable of generating activity.

Before computers, prospect information was kept in logs, leading to the phrase "a book of business." Some of our "sales ancestors" kept prospects on scraps of paper in a shoe box. Nowadays, most off the shelf CRM software has a feature that will enable the rep or their manager to view the entirety of a sales pipeline in several manners (i.e. adjusted by probability of closure, by closing date, by amount, etc.).

What I like is the ability to generate graphs or a visual pipeline funnel. Visual reminders of what you've sold as compared to your goals can be powerful. Create a visual for your pipeline and put it on the wall next to that motivating picture of the yacht, sports car or beach house so you remember that goal attainment is a result of keeping the pipeline full.

Whatever system you use, the point is you need a system! One of the greatest challenges for many reps is organization. Organization has an evil twin called "discipline." Applying these twin evils when viewing your sales pipeline as the embodiment of your business is the difference between success and failure. After all, to quote author Nathan Whitley, "The pain of regret is far greater than pain of discipline!"

Having and maintaining a sales pipeline is step one. Step two is understanding that your pipeline is always dynamic, constantly changing and can provide you with great information.

For example, let's say a rep has an annual quota of selling a million dollars of product and their sales cycle is three months. If they close about a third of what they put into the pipeline, then they may want to have somewhere between $750K and a million in their pipeline at any one time.

Here's how that math works: one third times three months means that about one-ninth of what is in the pipeline will close in any given month. Since 9 months equals three-quarters of a year, shoot for at least three quarters of the annual quota to be present.

If you're saying this is all statistical malarkey, remember that numbers don't lie – it's the people who use them or ignore them that do. You'll need to establish your own formulas for effectively using a pipeline approach to manage your sales business. What else can the understanding of your pipeline reveal?

Are all of your eggs in one basket? What if that one big sale you've invested countless weeks in falls through?

Are you getting any new business or just relying on repeat customers? I advocate for making customers, not sales. We do a lot of repeat of business, but our business only grows if we keep adding new people to turn into repeat customers.

Will your finances allow your mental state to be positive? When diligently maintained, your pipeline will reveal your future paychecks. It can answer if you have taken care to "pay yourself first." In other words, you know you've been busy, but have you been productive?

You can have loads of fulfillment issues, customer service items, administrative busywork and no time for lunch. But a quick glance at the pipeline will tell you if you have enough income projected over the next month to pay your mortgage. It can tell you if you have ample appointments set for next month's bills. Being productive means filling up the pipeline and closing deals. Don't confuse it with being busy.

Yes, a full pipeline can allow you to relax. It's a signal that you've been doing the right things. It helps you through the loss of a prospect because you know there are many others already working through your system.

Understanding and using a pipeline mentality is the difference between being *proactive* (that is, aggressively and responsibly filling up your pipeline) and *reactive* (i.e. hoping the phone rings and taking what comes your way). Ultimately, it is the difference between controlling your market or being controlled by it.

Most reps that are industry leaders understand that the key to sustaining big sales is a full pipeline.

Five Steps Deciding Your Commission

The Morgue
Sales World, Everywhere

I'll often hear the following from our salespeople: "I lost the "XYZ" sale." In fact, I've said it myself many times. Okay, sales troopers everywhere, time to be honest with ourselves. Can we really lose something we've never had?

We incorporated a sales training exercise into a two-day, company-wide meeting. The group was split into two teams, each trying to sell the same account. Two other staffers and I acted out the role of "client," while each team consisted of several salespeople and support staff.

Unbeknown to the teams, an elaborate, albeit fictitious, history was created for the client. Teams were judged on their discovery skills, their sales strategy, the product/solution they pitched, and their presentation. In preparation for the exercise, we had actually divided up points for each of these areas in hopes we'd convey their relative importance in the overall process.

Being a small group that had worked together for a long time, the jokes flowed, but to everyone's credit the exercise was taken quite seriously. In the end, it was clear that one team had designed the best solution. However, even the other judges were surprised when we summed up the scoring and found the team with the best solution didn't win the sale.

The team with the less impressive solution/design was awarded the contract because they won in the areas of discovery, strategy, and presentation. Overall, they heard what the "prospect" was trying to achieve, not just what the prospect said they had an in interest in initially purchasing. In short, they got it. Do you "get" what your customers are trying to achieve?

Another key to that training exercise was that if it were a real-life scenario, the losing team, which did have a stronger product solution, probably wouldn't have ever gotten that far in the process. They lost the client's confidence during the needs ascertainment process. How you uncover information plays a huge role in how you, and your company, are viewed by a prospect.

While it may not be fair, it is factual that when you go to meet a prospect for the first time, you are either benefiting greatly, or miserably burdened by that prospect's preconceived impression of your company or its products. What is the awareness-level and perception of your firm's products, services and abilities? What is your company doing to enhance those attributes on an ongoing basis?

When I worked for Group W Television it was far easier to get appointments with senior level management than it was when I was representing Syndicast. The former was known as an industry leader with innovative and successful products, whereas the latter had a reputation of selling "shlock."

The past few chapters of this book have been focused on why buyers buy. The individual chapters are necessarily interrelated. Professional salespeople face some of their biggest challenges when they encounter a prospect who has some of the pieces of the puzzle in place, but not all. A good example of this is the potential customer who is properly motivated but can't follow through. For example, the prospect has a clear need, but does not possess the ability to pay, rendering them worthless to the sales rep.

Note to reps everywhere: make sure all the pieces of the motivation puzzle are examined. We thrive on hope, but we hurt our wallets if we invest too much time in the wrong prospects.

Presuming you are a legitimate contender to furnish a particular product or service, here is another way of looking at the steps to client decision processes. These five hurdles are common to decision making whether you are selling b-to-b or directly to a consumer. While I like to think salespeople are masters of their own destiny, let's face facts: those prospects, and the decisions they make, do impact our pocketbooks.

Step One:

What does the customer think of *YOU?*

In some ways, it's a disservice to sales reps everywhere when a sales manager or trainer says, "It's not personal."

"Personal," in the sales vernacular, may not mean the same thing as in other truly personal relationships. But if a prospective client doesn't feel comfortable with you, the salesperson, there is very little chance a sale will be consummated.

Think of a simple shopping excursion to the mall. You may have an interest in a new shirt. While you're examining the shirt in the store, a salesperson working for the retailer approaches. If you are put off by their approach, their appearance, the things they say or do, it affects your decision. Even if you are enamored with the shirt, you know that every time you put it on, you'll be thinking of that salesperson. No sale.

Let's look at a business-to-business sales scenario. Remember that many businesses rely on what I call the "domino theory" (which is the non-MBA way of discussing supply chain economics). A business is reliant on its suppliers and its customers. If there is a drop off on either end, the whole thing can come crumbling down.

If your company sells machine parts, your buyers are relying on you to understand where and how your parts fit into their productivity. If you let them down, it shuts down production and endangers their relationship with their clients. Before they get to decide about your product, its price or your ability to fulfill their needs, that buyer is making judgments about you. It *is* personal.

Step Two:

What does the customer think of YOUR COMPANY?

I have several friends who are pharmaceutical sales reps. They work hard to maintain good relationships with physicians and the appropriate office staff in the doctor's offices where they make their sales calls. I've often wondered how their sales would be impacted if the company they worked for was found to have defective or dangerous products.

Even if the product line they represented was fine, what additional burdens of proof and sales hurdles would they have to climb through if their companies had reputations that weren't stellar?

I have an ad agency client with whom I've worked on a number of trade show projects over the years. They rely on their vendors to make them look good to their clients. In one year I sold them (and their clients) over $100,000 of product.

One particularly time-sensitive project seemed to be cursed with minor problems throughout the process. Ultimately, on the day production was complete, six of seven cases shipped out. One was left on the loading dock 2000 miles away.

Although we managed to make it right and all was invisible to their client, in the agency's mind there was now a question mark regarding our reliability. It was close to two years before I sold them another thing.

A company's image is blessed if their reputation is one of delivering quality service and standing by their products. Conversely, it's cursed if they are known for being difficult to work with and unreasonable when issues arise.

The company that is well known for a particular product or area of expertise may become pigeonholed. Reps selling for this company may have a hard time getting potential buyers to consider the company for new things since they are so associated with a particular product or service.

Several years ago, I was working with a company on a design for a tradeshow that was going to be their coming out party or "re-birth." The company made super expensive, high-end barbecue grills. Their problem was they had developed a horrendous reputation amongst their retail customers for not delivering on time. People loved the product, but the initial customers (the retailers) couldn't count on the manufacturer delivering.

The problem arose from too much demand and not enough production capacity. Their sales reps would meet with retail purchasing agents who were skeptical about placing orders and committing wholesale purchasing dollars for product they couldn't count on re-selling within a determined timeframe.

Is there anything about your company's reputation that is hurting your sales?

Step Three:

Does the customer believe you and your company UNDERSTAND THEIR NEEDS?

Congratulations. You've made it past two of the toughest hurdles. The prospect feels comfortable with you and your company. Now, don't blow it!

Several doors down from our old Greenville, South Carolina location is the local office of a nationwide cellular phone company. Frequently, I was contacted by some rep from their office asking for an appointment to learn about our company's telephone and mobile communication needs.

I generally declined for two reasons. One was due to lack of need. The second reason is the company had violated step number two. Their infraction was excessive rep turnover. No sooner would I get a call from a salesperson than the rep would be gone. It damaged the company in my mind. However, one time when they called, we had just finished an internal meeting and decided to consider revamping our cell phone policy in all five offices.

The rep, accompanied by a sales manager, showed up promptly for the meeting. They asked some good questions, took lots of notes, and stressed that they'd put together a *customized* solution as our five-office footprint in three states presented them with some unique challenges.

In under an hour, they were back! Because we were right next door, they wanted to drop off and review the proposal. My disappointment was palpable. How could they have dealt with our issues in less than an hour? Had they oversold the complexity of our perceived challenges? Did they forget that they had promised personalized solutions to our situation? Either way, I was skeptical as I opened the presentation.

My apprehension was well founded. They had simply filled in some blanks on a standard form and asked me to sign it. All credibility they had built through their company's multimillion-dollar advertising and their rep's approach during the "discovery" stage was now shot. They demonstrated that they either *didn't care* or *didn't understand* what we needed.

How are you conveying to your prospects that you and your company understand their needs?

Step Four:

What does the customer think of YOUR SOLUTION?

This is the part of the buying process where the rep's challenge is to connect the dots between the initial needs or desires stated by the customer and a proposed solution (product or service).

With any single buying decision, the prospect is considering the totality of the offer. While the product or service itself is the focus of their evaluation, issues such as warrantees, terms and conditions, delivery, service and repair may all play a role in how they view your "solution."

For instance, let's go back to the simple purchase of a shirt. Is the shirt that the salesperson is advocating the right solution for your expressed desire or need? Will it make you look the way you want to look? Is the texture right? Does it go with other clothing you've already decided on for a special occasion?

If that salesperson knew, as a result of proper discovery, that the shirt was for a special occasion or had to go with a particular outfit, they'd have a much better chance of advocating an acceptable solution.

Step Five:

What does the customer think of YOUR PRICE?

Although price always matters, unless you are dealing with a pure commodity item it is rarely the sole decision point. However, it is the most frequent excuse for not buying when one of the previous steps has not been successfully overcome.

If you want to learn a lot about your selling style, to improve your ability to sell, and to improve your income, try the following exercise. First, make a list of the last five (or ten) sales you thought you had a good shot at getting but couldn't close. Look at the five steps above. Be brutally honest with yourself and try to identify when you "lost" the sale.

If there is a pattern, addressing it and improving can lead to fatter commission checks in the future. Even if there isn't a pattern, using these five steps as a roadmap and litmus test for future prospects will help you achieve more big sales.

Usually, Nobody Dies!

High Tech Client
Raleigh, North Carolina

> *"More people would learn from their mistakes if they weren't*
> *so busy denying them." J.Harold Smith*

I have a friend who is a surgeon. If he has a bad day and makes a mistake, it could be fatal. In sales, when we make mistakes, the worst we do is kill a deal. No matter how important something may seem at the time, it's best to remember if you screw it up, the chances are your kids and spouse will still love you, the dog will wag its tail when he sees you come home, and most likely, nobody dies.

Sometimes when we look back on a lost deal, what we term a "mistake" was actually a deliberate decision that was not the correct one. A few years ago, one of our marketing consultants was developing a fairly large project with an existing client of hers. I screwed it up – or at least didn't help matters.

A fast growing I.T. company had been a client for about five years. Initially, our rep had worked with the founders. As the company grew, they took on layers of management that led to layers of workers in the trenches. The responsibility for the company's new custom tradeshow exhibit fell on a staffer in the marketing department. To me, he appeared to be more concerned with his role in the process and how he'd look to his boss rather than doing what was in the company's best interests.

Although our rep at one time had a direct relationship with the owners, their Director of Marketing had a personal relationship with one of our competitors. Their new Sales Manager also had influence on the project and his desires seemed in conflict with those of the marketing manager. At best, we were getting mixed signals. And worse, we were working with a lot of "influencers" who could say no, but we weren't in direct contact with the people who could say yes.

However, it appeared as though we were making progress. The staffer shared with us that he had ruled out several companies vying for the business and we just needed to take our cues from him as to how to win the account. The sole remaining competitor, as it turned out, was the friend of the Director of Marketing.

Because of all the voices influencing the creative, functional or financial aspects of the project, we were asked to make numerous revisions to our proposal. Each one essentially cost us time and money. Then, everything seemed to hit a wall. We couldn't reach our contact. We weren't getting the feedback that had been so plentiful along the way. Our marketing consultant had a lot invested in the project. She was feeling both the pressures she'd put on herself and that of her sales manager. We strategized on approaches to get the deal closed as the last thing we were told was they were likely buying our solution. The last thing our contact had stressed was to stick with him and not to try to go around him for an answer.

Well, if the same tactic worked in every situation, I guess sales really would be easy and we'd all be rich. After determining that the marketing director was likely allied with her friend and our contact was low-level, we made the decision to contact the owners (with whom we had a pre-existing relationship) "indirectly" by copying them on correspondence with our contact. Instantly, we lost the ability to remain in contention.

Did I make a mistake or a judgment call? I didn't want to keep pouring resources into a losing situation and didn't want to be used so the marketing director could just get a better deal from her friend. We had earned the right to be dealt with fairly. But in the end, we didn't make the sale.

Was the mistake going around our contact? Was the mistake forcing our rep to take action when patience was called for? Was the mistake not recognizing the strength of the relationship between the Director of Marketing and our competition earlier?

I make lots of mistakes. Most of them are judgment calls that don't work out. I'm far more successful because I prefer to make a mistake than spend my life on a fence. I'm not afraid to make mistakes because usually, nobody dies.

Somewhere out there is a pharmaceutical sales rep that sold the Tylenol that some nut poisoned which killed people. The rep sold something that led to death. Does that mean they shouldn't make more sales? Of course not! It wasn't their doing that led to death.

The only time a sales rep is responsible in the event of catastrophe is if they knowingly represent a harmful, substandard product. The rep who sells elevator equipment to high-rise construction projects isn't liable if there is an accident. However, if the rep *knows* the elevator's brake system is substandard and hides that fact, there is most definitely culpability.

One of the last things I tell a new sales rep as their initial training concludes is that it's okay to make a mistake. I just don't want them making the same mistake twice! Mistakes are learning opportunities and the profession of sales is best practiced by those committed to continual learning. Making a mistake is fine. Making the same mistake twice is stupid.

When a mistake is made there usually is a consequence. You may lose the sale. How you respond and react to a mistake, however, may determine if you lose the customer. Usually, a client will understand that mistakes happen. What they expect is for a vendor to understand how their mistake have impacted the customer.

For instance, if you sell a machine part to a customer who relies on you to keep their production line going and you order the wrong part that won't fit, have you shut down their production line? Have you compromised their ability to service their customers in a timely fashion? Do you appreciate the chain of events your mistake set into motion?

As a sales rep, you are often in the position of accepting responsibility for mistakes made by others. You are the public face of your organization to the client. But there are also mistakes of your own creation. Did you oversell a service? Did you make product claims that were guess work – and guessed wrong?

When a problem occurs, remember the story of "Chicken Little." When an acorn went "kerplunk!" on Chicken Little's head in the forest, she thought the sky was falling. It was an overreaction to something that happened. Reps must discern between dealing with stuff that happens and a true crisis. Keep things in perspective.

Blowing a sale or even losing a customer is bad. It'll hurt you financially. Make too many and you may lose your job, your home, and your self-reliance. Paint the worst scenario and stretch it out. Now look back at the mistake and put it in perspective. Most likely, nobody died.

Attitudinal Self-Perceptionectomy

WNRW-TV
Greensboro, NC

L ong before I moved South, (one never becomes a Southerner, you are either born to it or you hear a lot of, "you're not from here, are you?"), I would travel throughout the region on business. My Northern mentality included a jaded sense of weather. It wouldn't matter what the forecasters said, if I was going South, it would be warm in my book.

On one trip, the car service picked me up to take me to the airport. The blizzard in the Northeast was of little concern, as I knew I was heading South, to the warmth. I certainly didn't have need of my woolen overcoat. Wrong.

When my flight landed in Greensboro, NC I met up with Charlie, my sales manager who had flown down on a separate flight. I was also met by the worst snowstorm the Triad region had seen in years. At the time, there were four television stations in the market, and we had appointments with all of them that day. Or, at least, that was the plan.

This was my first co-call with Charlie, who was new to the company. He was very much the stickler for establishing good sales habits and following them, regardless of any impediments Mother Nature threw his way. Charlie insisted I drive, since I'd be driving if he wasn't there. So, I drove to the appointment, parked in their nearly empty "snow day" lot, and started to get out of the car.

"Wait a minute," he bellowed. "Don't you want to prepare for the meeting?" I answered that I had researched the stations' ratings over the previous weekend and reviewed them on the plane. I knew where they may have a need for our programs and which of their co-owned stations in other markets planned to purchase our shows. He said, "All that's good, but where's your head at? How's your attitude?"

Charlie understood that prior to going into any meeting, it was important to perform what over the years I've come to call an "attitudinal self-perceptionectomy." The medical dictionaries don't classify this procedure. Your sales manual should.

Take everything that is going on in your world and the larger world around you and shut it out. Get your head focused on the meeting about to take place. The next few minutes effect your income. Before going into battle (a sales call), the valiant warrior (you) must be prepared.

Preparation isn't just doing your research and having the proper brochures or product samples. It's mental. It's feeling good. It will be evident in your posture, your tonal quality, the vigor in your walk and the sincerity of your handshake. In a word, it's attitude!

Your attitude is wholly transparent to most customers. Are you going to be perceived as a peddler out to sell your stuff, or a trusted supplier with an interest in your prospect's success? The customer with whom you are about to meet doesn't want to hear about your problems at home or the things in your work life that aggravate you (especially your complaints about other customers).

Your prospect wants to deal with an energized, enthusiastic problem-solver. You are the only one who can control the attitude you take into your next sales call. Be sure to perform an attitudinal self-perceptionectomy – because how you perceive yourself will impact how they perceive you.

If you know you're down, somewhere between the front door and the receptionist's desk you better get pumped up! If you are feeling desperate to make a sale, put on a mask that will hide the desperation and bring out the benefits you offer. If you are feeling like a loser, find a way to laugh and put forward a winner's attitude when with the client.

During a lunch break at an all-day Group W sales meeting we got into an informal "true confessions" of what each of the reps did to get themselves "psyched" prior to walking into a sales call. The answers ranged from prayer, to blasting music, to vigorous isometric exercise, to one rep who called the receptionist a few minutes before each meeting so that she'd be greeted by name when she walked into the lobby. Being greeted by name in a strange place helped pump her up and improved her self-perception.

Since you were a child, you've heard the importance of "attitude." When you were a spoiled-rotten, cranky kid, your parents told you your attitude stunk. Perhaps your high school coach told you you'd never go far with a lazy attitude. Maybe your attitude has also messed up some of your adult relationships.

As in life, attitude matters in sales. It will determine how much you sell. If your prospect senses you have a lousy attitude pre-sale, what can they expect in the way of service after the sale? Ultimately, they perceive what effort you put into gaining their business. And in sales, like so many other aspects of life, you get out of it what you put into it!

The best way to focus on growing your sales is to focus on your client's success. It's the difference between an approach that begins with "what can I sell you" and a relationship that starts with "how may I help you?" The difference is more than just the approach. The difference is attitude. How do they perceive you? How do you perceive yourself?

The other area of your sales world where attitude matters is in your relationships with co-workers, colleagues, managers and subordinates. Most will co-exist with a rep that has a lousy attitude if they are performing. But few will do anything more than the bare minimum to help them. However, an unselfish, cooperative attitude can yield miracles when it comes to support and assistance. Both are necessary for you to reach your potential. So, be sure to perform a periodic 'attitudinal self-perceptionectomy" as it relates to your co-workers, not just your clients.

A positive attitude can make the difference between a winner and loser. It can make the difference between doing okay and kicking ass. Every rep has a hidden switch inside their heads. It takes a conscientious effort to flip that switch. In one direction, the switch is labeled, "I'll try." In the other direction, the switch is labeled, "I will!"

Don't try to do better than last year. Make the absolute decision that you *will* sell more than last year. Don't try to hit your quota. Make the decision that you *will* hit your quota. Don't allow for failure to be an option. Make the decision that success is your destiny and your inalienable right! It's attitude.

Sales is a tough business. It's a risk-reward proposition. Your attitude will help combat the opposition which comes in the face of competition, market forces, world events, timing, budget cycles and the ever-present challenges inherent with any type of human interaction. You need every possible advantage to succeed. Attitude is one thing you and you alone control – so use it to your advantage.

When I had worked at Group W for several years, Ned Goldstein, the president of the division, was chatting with some people outside my office one Friday afternoon. While others were in a jovial, entering-the-weekend state of mind, I was obviously stressed, melancholy, concerned and staring at the telephone. He cajoled me to come out into the hall and share what was on my mind.

It had started about six months earlier in Tallahassee, Florida. While there on a sales trip, I discovered a local teacher recognition project that a TV Station had been doing. It brought together on-air broadcast elements, community outreach and sponsorship opportunities. It was a local example of the kind of project our group syndicated nationally.

I approached my management about developing the Florida station's campaign on a national level. The thought of market-leading broadcasters teaming up to recognize teacher excellence was enticing. Then, we built on the concept by organizing a national conference that brought together these top teachers to share tactics and ideas.

We got the White House involved and held a ceremony to kick things off at The Kennedy Center. To add legs to the project, we teamed up with leading non-profit groups involved in improving education as well as groups dedicated to public-private partnerships that promoted educational excellence. But before all this could take place, we had to sell the project to both a commercial sponsor and to broadcasters throughout the country.

The folks on our team responsible for lining up the sponsor struck a deal with Apple Computer to sponsor the project on a national scale. The nationwide rollout was contingent on a successful pilot year in about twenty-five markets which had to include three specific cities of strategic importance to Apple. In other words, if we didn't get broadcasters in those key cities, no $7 million deal!

In most markets, those of us responsible for selling the stations had no problems. The project was an all-around win. However, Atlanta, one of the must-have markets, was giving us a problem. In addition to feeling responsible for the program as a whole since I had developed it, I was the account executive in charge of the Atlanta market.

It wasn't that there wasn't interest among the stations – there just wasn't need or room. One station that was interested was too weak for Apple to be happy. They needed a station with a big signal. I needed the station with the big signal to say yes.

I remember Ned asking about the approaches I had taken to selling the project to an Atlanta station and my reassuring all that could be done had been done. He inquired about the response our overtures had received. Finally, he asked if the passion now evident in my worry was there in my presentations. He felt it had to be. Otherwise, if I hadn't put everything I had into the process, I'd be feeling guilty, not antsy.

He reminded me that if I took a winner's attitude into sales situations the likelihood of walking out a winner was that much greater. Then, the phone rang. My sales assistant told me the General Manager from WSB-TV, Atlanta was on the line. This was the moment of truth. Months of hard work and millions of dollars of revenue were riding on the outcome of this conversation.

I told those assembled outside my office not to be offended if I shut the door. After a moment of pleasantries, Barry, the GM, indicated he needed to make the call quick. His weekend was supposed to have started at noon and he was running late, but he wanted me to have a good weekend. He then informed me that WSB would carry the "Thanks To Teachers" campaign!

Before hanging up, he said one other thing, "Steve, one of the things that sold it was your attitude about this project. You showed us it is important and beneficial and that you guys will do it right."

In pursuit of big sales, there is no substitute for a positive attitude!

Two Ears – One Mouth – Use Proportionately

Syndicast Services
New York, NY

There is a disturbing myth that salespeople need to be good talkers. It's not that it's not true. I'd just more accurately say that salespeople need to be good communicators. And communication is a two-way street.

Later in this book, I'll address communication issues dealing with comprehension and understanding (i.e. "Is what you said what they heard?" and "Is what they said what you heard?"). Here, I'm simply examining the necessity for more listening and less talking. Here are some reasons why.

First of all, when you, the sales rep, are speaking, you are not learning anything about your client's needs, desires, preferences, time schedules, budgets or intentions.

When you go into a pitch without having gone through a proper needs ascertainment or discovery process, it's far too easy to be selling a 'watch-a-ma-callit" when the prospect really needed a "thig-a-ma-jiggy."

As small children, we are told not to speak in class, in the library, or when others are talking. As we get older, we still aren't supposed to talk to strangers. As adults, some people love to talk but may not be given the chance. Sometimes, you can be a hero to your customers just by giving them the opportunity to speak.

In sales, it is said that there is nothing sweeter for a prospect than hearing their own name. I'd suggest hearing their own voice ranks right up there, as well as being given the opportunity to share thoughts and made to feel that their opinion matters.

Indeed, one of the best ways to sell is to get the prospect to "sell themselves." People like to buy, but few like to be sold. If the voice they are hearing is their own, the sound may be familiar and the message credible. That's not possible if you're the one talking.

Another reason reps need to speak less and listen more is that our prospects may tell us exactly how to sell to them. If we learn that the reason they are looking at a new vendor is because of delivery problems with their current source, wouldn't it make sense to focus on your firm's excellent delivery record?

In my sales management career selling trade show exhibits, I've seen many reps waste precious facetime with clients because they are too anxious to pitch the benefits of a particular product. Clients come to us wanting something new. Then the rep blows it by pitching something identical to what the client already owns and wants to replace. If only the reps had listened more and talked less!

When you feel somebody cares about you or takes an interest in you, there is a greater tendency to aim your business their way. Reps need to realize that instilling those feelings in prospects has more to do with being a good listener than being the one doing the talking.

One side benefit to the industry I'm in is I get exposed to business-to-business interactions at a fast and furious pace at trade shows. Several years ago, I was in NY attending "Internet World" at the Jacob Javits center. Think of old movies and how they portray a middle eastern open-air market. This was the same thing, but instead of people selling fruit, rice and vegetables, they were hyping the latest dot-com wares.

When it comes to the intricacies of computer software or hardware, I may as well have been on Mars and not Manhattan. It was another language being spoken and not one to which I could easily assimilate. A typical conversation between me and a salesperson in a booth would go like this:

Me: (stone silence)

Them: Hi! How's your Lan/Wan Server interface modulation capacity app?

Me: (?)

Them: Here's how it works. Data converts to analog fluctuation with transmission recession at bips and mips you wouldn't believe!

Had the booth staffer not insisted on talking to me without learning that I wasn't a prospect, they could have instead talked with one of the four other real prospects walking past the booth while we were "speaking." It is only by listening to prospective clients that we can learn if they are candidates for our products and services.

I had been practicing for weeks learning all there was to know about a new project that Syndicast was about to launch. It was a package of TV programs and sponsorable vignettes celebrating the US Constitution (this wasn't shlock). It was my turn to role-play or "do the pitch" for Ben Kitch, the president of Syndicast, before I went out to the real world in hopes of making a sale.

In retrospect, either the man had the patience of a saint or it was easy enough for him to feign listening because he had a large TV in his office with a Cable Business News channel (sound off) that was scrolling throughout our session. We started with the obligatory "fake" chit chat that is designed to replicate reality in a role play situation, then led to some carefully scripted opening remarks I'd prepared.

And then I delved into the meat of the presentation, going on and on until I concluded the mock-presentation. I even remembered to ask for the order! I was exhilarated I had remembered the details – all of them!

Ben said, "You were perhaps the most thorough of any rep who has pitched this to me. You also managed to talk non-stop for forty-five minutes without ever involving me in your sales process." It was then that my exhilaration departed.

I make many references in this book to how "the interview process" is similar to a sales pitch. The product is you. I do this because it is a universal sales encounter that virtually all readers can identify with.

I have no idea what the future holds for me and if or when I'll be interviewing for a job somewhere. For the time being, I'm on the hiring side of the desk. If after someone's first interview with me I recognize I've done the bulk of the talking, that person most definitely gets invited back! Here's why:

Sales managers need to know their reps are asking good questions. The manner in which you ask questions can often set you apart from your competition – that, and listening to the answers!

Note to reps everywhere: pay attention to this equation. Two ears, one mouth. Use proportionately!

Health Matters

Reds
Dayton, Ohio

Greenville, South Carolina has been a great place to live and raise our family. Coming to the area from another world, (New York) I can appreciate much of what the region offers in terms of social, environmental and business opportunities. I've been accused of being a walking Chamber of Commerce poster (you can learn about this wonderful place and the hundreds of national and international accolades its received at www.yeahthatgreenville.com). So, I was shocked to read that a deodorant company had once done a study of 100 metropolitan areas and found Greenville to be the country's second sweatiest city! (You folks in El Paso had us beat.)

The study examined the percentage of overweight people in a region combined with that region's heat and humidity. They didn't fly around the nation checking out people's arm pits. Sweating is a natural biological response to help keep cool and regulate the body's temperature. But what about excessive sweating?

We all know someone (even if you don't live in Greenville or El Paso) who seems to always be perspiring. Most likely, your preference is not to sit next to that person in the car pool or at a crowded lunch counter.

What about the person with the ever-present smoker's cough? You know, the one who hacks up throaty sounds in the middle of their own sentences and doesn't even notice? Is your impression of them one that says, "They are somebody I want to spend time with?"

Now think of the frustration you have with that colleague of yours who seems to have a sick day on a recurring basis. They are the ones who catch every cold, always have a migraine, just generally feel weak and "can't get to work."

Unhealthy behavior is a turn-off as well. All of us have met "the exaggerator" who knows super important people or has been responsible for most of the progress known to western mankind. Is this not a plea for attention? Do you feel comfortable trusting and interacting with this person?

It seems that on a daily basis there are new studies and reports in the media telling us America's youth is obese and their parents are equally unhealthy. In the business world, appearance matters. In the business world, "health" matters.

Athletes and performers know that to be at their peak performance it is imperative to be in shape and stay in shape. So many things are beyond a salesperson's control (including genetics) but the choice to make good health both a goal and a habit is a conscientious decision. Choose health.

Before going on, let me stress that when I refer to health or illness in this chapter I'm not writing about the unfortunate victim of a serious illness. Rather, I'm referring to the vast numbers of us who ignore both the obvious and the empirical data that health is a pre-requisite to sustaining high levels of performance.

To put it simply, when we get sick and feel lousy we are rarely at our best. What if feeling tired, drained, and strained was your natural state of being?

Reps need to have energy. Without it, the hours they work suffer. Without it, their personality fades. Without it, the numbers of clients they see diminishes. Reps need energy to invigorate presentations. Reps need energy to ignite passion.

Reps need energy for the physical requirements of their jobs, whether those requirements are simply hammering at a keyboard, dialing a phone, or digging deep to find that last smile after a long day.

Reps need mental energy, too. Good reps in most fields are aggressive thinkers. Without mental energy, creativity pales. Rather than taking new approaches to old, resistant prospects, we approach them with a defeatist attitude because its easier. Without mental energy the conduit from our ears to our brains gets clogged. We make mistakes and lose sales.

Good health effects both our present performance and our longevity. Some companies don't want to keep the chronically ill on the payroll. Rising insurance premiums are of major concern to employers large and small. Longevity is often a key ingredient to salespeople who are comfortable in a career rather than bouncing from job to job.

If you recognize yourself in the examples described in this chapter, there is a good chance prospects may not want to spend time with you. Do you want to be coughed and hacked at? Do you want to be locked in the tiny conference room with Ms. or Mr. Sweat? Do you want to trust your business to someone who is often out sick?

Whether it is a matter of appearance, ability, perception or concentration, health matters.

I flew into Dayton, Ohio for a meeting with a TV station Program Director. It was our first acquaintance and he insisted on buying me lunch (usually, the sales rep buys). He was an old timer who had grown up in business and savored the tradition of the three martini lunch.

At that time, lunch for me was often a trip to the salad bar or a frozen yogurt after a workout at the gym. He bemoaned the fact that, in his words, he had become a "piranha" for enjoying an alcoholic beverage before happy hour.

The same "piranha" or "outcast" label is now sticking to smokers. Even in many parts of tobacco-dependent agricultural states, lighting up is viewed as a no-no. Whether or not a salesperson chooses to forego cigarettes for health reasons, plain economics and common sense should ward you off the evil cancer sticks.

I have sent away sales reps who called on me within seconds of their arrival simply because they stink. The fact that you put out your cigarette before entering the building does not diminish the stench you carry into a sales appointment on your clothing, your breath and your sales samples.

You sell more by not putting negatives into a buyer's mind. If a rep's attitude about their personal health and/or hygiene is in question, why would a prospect desire to spend time or do business with the rep? Perceptions matter.

Health matters. Not only will you feel better, you'll sell more!

Ooze And Exude!

TV Station Boardroom
Tri-Cities, TN

When a cute, friendly puppy licks your face, you know it's excited to see you. You are motivated to reach out and scratch its ears or rub its belly. That dog has sold you on petting it!

Chances are, you didn't stand a chance. Especially if you're a repeat customer for the hound, it knows how to appeal to you. The dog expresses interest in you. "Puppy love" takes on a new form as you, the prospect, are showered with attention, warmth, and perhaps some gentle prodding. Moreover, it's all done by a "sales-puppy" who is 100% into what they are doing, totally focused on pleasing you, and full of playful energy!

So, should we all show up to our next client meeting on all fours with a leash on our necks and lick the prospect? I imagine there are some body-piercing salesmen and goth jewelry reps where that may be appropriate. However, for most of us, we'll be better off excelling at human interaction rather than emulating our canine friends.

When was the last time that you walked out of a client pitch knowing you had bubbled over with authentic enthusiasm for whatever it is you sell? The answer should be, "The last time I left a client pitch!" Let's look at several reasons enthusiasm is a major ingredient to big sales.

First of all, without it, you are a drag to be with. Who wants to spend time with a drag? Who wants to buy a product or service from a drag? Who wants to think of the drag whenever they use the item they may or may not purchase from a drag?

This book deals with reality. The only "theories" I share are based on my personal experiences. The following is not a cosmic, ethereal, new age, space age, left or right brained freaky theory. It is just another observation. In fact, I think I'm paraphrasing some scientifically-proven law. But, for our purposes, let's call it the Law of Energy.

Hoffman's Law of Energy states, "Some folks are downers. Some are positive. The downers can suck the life out of otherwise energetic, happy people. Conversely, positive energy transfers to those around it, increasing interest, attention span, desire to associate and willingness to cooperate."

Energy is something that comes from within and emanates outward. Make sure what you are putting out there is positive. Here are some ways to minimize being negative in your sales life:

- Avoid negative people, because they will bring you down!
- Avoid disorganization, because if you're never on top of your game – you'll never be on top of your game.
- Avoid being late, because you can never re-capture time.
- Avoid exhaustion – when you're run down its easier to get run over.
- Avoid narrow mindedness, because when you believe you know it all and stop showing an interest in learning new things, it's insulting to others around you.
- Avoid sharing your crisis du jour.
- Avoid bringing the world's problems into your clients' home or office – bring in a positive news story instead!

Why else is oozing and exuding enthusiasm over your product and service so important? Who knows more about your stuff than you? Your prospect is expecting their sales rep to be an expert on the product. You may also be expected to be an expert in your industry.

If you are meeting with someone who views you as the expert, and you are also totally up and positive, the likelihood is they will be open to hearing whatever it is you offer. Now, take that thinking to the next step.

Once you discover their needs or desires, and the time comes to present your solution/pitch, if they see "the expert" is totally psyched about how well this proposed solution will meet their needs, then they are that much more likely to buy it.

From the buyer's perspective, it's the difference between a sales guy going through the motions and a rep with their best interests at heart (i.e. "He's *pumped up excited* about how his stuff is meeting my needs. Man, if he's excited and he knows what he's talking about then I'm getting excited, too!")

Want another reason to stay energized at work? Without personally staying positive, how can your support team be expected to rally around you? If a support staff has a choice of devoting their time to helping build a positive rep's sales or "doing what they have to do" to assist an "un-enthusiastic" rep, enthusiasm will win every time!

In his inaugural address in January of 1989, the first President George Bush spoke of a theme he'd used throughout his campaign called "A Thousand Points of Light." The reference was to promote volunteerism and a greater sense of caring in our country.

At that time, I was working for Group W and we were launching a station image campaign called "Time to Care." The unpaid national endorsement of our President and the frequent press surrounding his "Thousand Points of Light" initiatives both during the campaign and after the inauguration was free publicity for the project. Sales took off.

Our reps in the Group W Target Marketing Group barnstormed the country. We would yank at the heartstrings of our prospects with energy and conviction. We sold with the passion of preachers and the belief of the most devout followers. The details were secondary to presentation. By the time we were done telling our (TV station) prospects that they'd be at the forefront of their communities, leading by example, all the while being more efficient in their own operations and instilling pride in their staffs and attracting new corporate dollars looking for a way to reach these thousand points of light, they were eager to sign on the dotted line.

As if on cue, two years later Group W was launching another TV station image project called "Celebrate America!" We introduced the project at a TV Programming convention. Our exhibition booth had numerous offices and screening rooms as well as a few large-screen TV's in the open spaces.

It was eerie. I came out of a screening room after meeting with a client and our booth was packed. Not just heavy-business busy, but shoulder-to-shoulder, not a spare square inch of space busy. Crowds numbering in the hundreds were surrounding our big TVs which were now tuned to CNN. America had just entered the Gulf War and the world was witnessing live television coverage of the first US Airforce bomb strikes.

In the following weeks America had much to be proud of. We began the sales campaign for the "Celebrate America" project just as U.S. Soldiers said goodbye to their loved ones in airports. Our sales push continued months later as some of these heroes came home. The sentiment and patriotism was palpable. It was once again, courtesy of President Bush, easy to turn a sales presentation into an emotional, enthusiastic, prideful pitch.

One memorable stop along that sales launch was in the town of Tri-Cities, Tennessee (and across the street, Tri-Cities, Virginia). This city was memorable for two reasons. The first was that I received a standing ovation in a board room sales presentation – I'd been applauded in public speaking engagements, but that is a different scenario than giving a pitch.

Perhaps it was the patriotism that was rampant at the time? Perhaps it was the carefully crafted sales pitch combining product benefits, localism, national pride, timeliness, and profits, all set against a background of outstanding Ray Charles music? But when you get a standing ovation in the process of asking for the order, it's usually a strong buying signal!

The other memorable thing would be a funny story, if it weren't so pathetic and true. It seems one of the TV stations in this market had just moved into a new facility. The owner of a competing TV station in town had a long-time rivalry (both personal and professional) with the first station.

Taking advantage of the war, the owner of the second station put on his National Guard uniform late one night when he knew the first station's only personnel would be one or two broadcast engineers manning the control room. On this dark, rainy night a loud and urgent pounding was heard by the control room engineer who hurried to see who was banging on the door.

He sees a man in uniform who says, "Open up, official business. Guard inspection of Public Media during war time." Well, this wasn't ethical, legal or moral. But he apparently said it with enough enthusiasm and conviction that he was let into the station and given a tour of his competitor's facility.

Admittedly, selling a television show where you have incredible visuals and energized music to add punch to your presentation may be easier than selling an industrial commodity product. But I've worked with enough passionate business people across a broad spectrum of industries to know it can be done.

One of the most mundane products I've encountered in my time with Skyline is a company that makes the stuff that goes into the "balls" of ball-point pens. Louis, the former owner, beseeched me to come and tour their factory to get a better understanding of their product.

In fact, it was a running joke for Louis that he had the "best balls" in the industry. Everyone loved "his balls." His enthusiasm for his product made me want to travel the few hours to see his balls. After all, we were hoping to sell him a display to "make his balls bigger than life!"

Actually, I was fascinated by the process. There was a "clean room" that would rival that of any high-tech computer fiber facility or medical laboratory. I learned that over 97% of Louis's business came from about 7 customers throughout the world. His balls kept the world's ink rolling through pens around the globe. They were quite successful, and subsequently the company was sold to a larger corporation.

The reality is that Louis's "balls" were very small. Dozens of them could fit on a fingertip. But the size of his enthusiasm for his product was enormous, and a key aspect to his big sales.

I'm Serious, You Gotta Laugh

United Nations
New York City

66 **L** augh and the world laughs with you. Weep and you weep alone." This quote, authored by Ella Wheeler Wilcox, seems like a decent start for a sales plan. Sales can't be done alone. At the very least, you need a buyer and a seller. Preferably, fewer sellers and lots of buyers.

Salespeople should have great senses of humor. After all, you get to take the blame for production screw ups. You get to take the blame for administrative screw ups. You get to take the blame for shipping screw ups. You get to take the blame when your support team doesn't provide adequate service or is unresponsive. So far, sounds like a laugh-a-minute job.

Want more? You get to take the blame when your client disavows your advice. You get to take the blame when your customer provided you with incorrect specifications. You become the villain who didn't deliver before the natural disaster, who delayed things, and who is the sole reason a shipment is stuck in customs. Damn, this job is a knee-slapper!

Are you using Skype or GoToMeeting for a videoconference? Or, even in person, good thing there's never a technical glitch!

How about the good clean yuks when you fly halfway across the country for a presentation, show up to your appointment, and your prospect decided to go boat shopping for the day? Or maybe you only had to drive across town, but your client had "put you down" on their calendar for the previous week? (Great to know they felt the appointment was so important they never bothered to call to see why you didn't show.)

Part of what makes all of this so much fun is that many of us salespeople have no salary and rely on commissions! It just makes it that much more of a laugh-out-loud riot when things blow up in your face!

Here's a good one: what about the rep who has such a good feeling about a super big sale that they neglect keeping their pipeline full and put all of their eggs in one basket. Their prospect has all but assured them of the order. Long days turn into weeks and then into two or three months working a major deal. After all, the prospect is the rep's best friend – it's in the bag. Then, the bag breaks, the best friend is fired, the project gets cancelled and the rep has no commissions coming in. I can just see you grinning ear-to-ear!

Which joke do you like better? The one where the customer shows up with their spouse to pick up their purchase and the spouse hates it so the customer tells the salesperson they got it all wrong? Or the 27-page request-for-proposal that shows up and with precise detail enumerates verbatim your competitor's product line and specs – then gives you all of 24 hours to respond?

Doing business with government agencies can be a real hoot. I had to laugh when a state law enforcement agency (who also had oversight for white collar crime) asked me to take an order and break our invoice into multiple increments of $2,499 since they could only charge $2,500 at a time on their credit card. Without doing that, they'd have to go to a competitive bid.

Exactly how should a rep react when they've sold several large (non-military and non-essential) projects to the Air Force and Navy, but everything comes to a halt because of a silly thing like a war! And isn't it fun when after months of working with a small local municipality to make a sale, the client's *absolute need* date is fast-approaching and they confirm you have the order, but, "Oh! The mayor is the only one authorized to sign for that, and she'll be back from her honeymoon in a month."

Or maybe you've just spent 4 months selling the legitimate product differences to your end-user contacts and then a procurement officer who knows nothing about the item in question buys the lowest of the bids – even though you were told your "sole source" application was perfect?

Do you enjoy the sales jollies inherent when a blurry fax hides a comma or decimal point and hundreds of the wrong item get delivered? If you want more international ha-has, just speak with any reps burned by mistakes in converting to or from the metric system, or those screwed by floats and fluctuations in currency exchanges.

Gosh this sales stuff is fun! Did I mention the part about no salary?

Volumes are written about and caricatures abound of traveling salesmen. I say we take all the jokes about missed kid's birthdays, missed anniversaries and more importantly, just missed time together, and put them in one big laugh bag. Then, let's take all the jokes about your presentation that was checked as baggage in Denver while you and your meeting are in Dallas and put them in another laugh bag. For roll-out-of-your-chair laughter, throw in the health problems and wrecked marriages.

For one last little giggle, remember it's not only your own family's finances that are on the line. You also shoulder the burden of keeping your company afloat. What a 'pissa' – all those jobs relying on you! You've got to be able to laugh.

Sales means there is pressure. Laughter is a release of pressure, a way to help you emotionally, mentally, even physically stay on an even keel in the midst of the highs and lows inherent in the position.

I am not advocating that all reps seek to become stand-up comics. In fact, many reps hurt themselves by coming off as Jerry Seinfeld, Chris Rock, Terri Gaffigan or Dat Phan (pick your laughter). In trying to be a comedian, there is the danger you'll abuse a prospect's time with jokes or stories, or even violate some well-defined lines in the sand that shouldn't be crossed.

Jokes and stories containing racial or ethnic humor simply have no place in the workplace. As funny as some may be, and as free of malice as the jokester may intend, you just never know who is married to or was raised by the exact people you're joking about. Sexual humor, too, should be restricted in your sales world. Do you really know whether or not the new prospect you're meeting is also a minister at their church? Do you want to risk the sale?

Political humor, too, is a dicey subject in the sales world. Yes, orders have been lost and even revoked after being placed by buyers who learn that the sales rep is a supporter of the wrong candidate or political party. Here in our little town of Greenville, SC, politics run deep. At one point, of the two largest ad agencies in town, the owner of one was the state chairman for the Democratic Party, and principals of the other have had both President Bushes at their homes. Doing business with both agencies, I'm keeping my mouth shut on political jokes!

Then, some people are just plain delusional. They can't have an encounter (even if you saw them the day before) without starting the conversation with a one-liner. As a sales professional, your integrity, and your prospect's comfort with you, are of the utmost importance. Chances are that the always-on, high-energy "wise-cracker" is being perceived by prospects as smarmy, lacking substance, and possibly untrustworthy as a vendor partner.

Sometimes the "Murphy" in Murphy's Law gets ahold of a sales opportunity. Murphy's Law states that if anything can go wrong, it will. Without laughter, Murphy wins and you lose. Without the ability to laugh, people won't want to be with you. In sales, that means you lose.

Sinclair Broadcast Group is now a huge corporation owning many stations and program affiliates. Back when they only owned three television stations, I was selling a fantastic half-hour comedy series which was actually an adult puppet show created and produced by Sid and Marty Krofft. The show, called *DC Follies,* was set in a mythical Washington D.C. bar where all of the regulars were well-known politicians, entertainers, correspondents or sports figures.

I had opened the Columbus, Ohio market for the project, and Sinclair's station there wanted the show badly. I had also been to Pittsburgh where Sinclair had a station, but we had a good deal in place with a much stronger station there. Now, I was in Baltimore at their station which was run by the head of the company. He wanted the show, too.

The problem was he wanted it for all of their stations, and I wasn't willing to do that deal. The sales call became surreal. In 1960 at the United Nations Russian Premiere Nikita Krushchev is said to have taken off his shoe and pounded on a desk to make a point. I was now staring at my own private Nikita.

The man was large and red in the face. He took off his shoe and pounded on his desk, demanding the series be sold to him in all his markets.

Do you fight and argue? Do you cower in terror?

Hell no, you just gotta laugh!

Ask What You Can Do For Others

In researching another chapter of this book, I looked for the website of Medstar Television, my old employer in Allentown, Pennsylvania. Courtesy of Google, I wound up with hundreds of thousands of "Meds" to scroll through.

Eventually, I found a listing for Medstar Television. It was a picture on someone's website indicating "at the Medstar luncheon." Like most industries, television programmers have their own conventions or "markets" where sellers showcase their wares, meet with clients and strengthen contacts. Cannes, France is the home to MipCom, a major market for international program sales.

The picture found in my Google search was from the website of a company called Cable Ready which was founded by Barry Lido. I first met Barry in the early or mid-eighties when I worked with Rachel Baugh, his wife at DL Taffner/Ltd. I recall contacting Barry when I learned he had left Columbia Pictures TV to start his own niche distribution company.

I was excited over his concept for taking existing programming libraries and representing/selling them to the growing number of cable outlets hungry for content. At that time, I was working for Medstar. I cannot recall if I first contacted him to wish him well, to explore the possibility of a job in the future, or to set him up with Medstar's owners to explore a business relationship.

Barry paid us a visit in Allentown. I was anxious to learn what he could do for us and shared that thought with Medstar's founder. He scowled and said, "This guy is trying to get a business off the ground. How about focusing instead on what we can do to help him."

I can't help but think that this was the attitude that led to Medstar's success over the years. And it does lead to building solid relationships. The picture I googled was of Saul Towlig, Medstar's co-founder, and Barry Lido, who was successfully representing Medstar Programming. There they were, many years after the initial Allentown meeting, enjoying lunch and celebrating success in the South of France.

I was organizing the grand opening of a newly-expanded office for The Oliver Group in Charlotte, NC. One of our Marketing Consultants urged me to meet with a gentleman named Randy Teller who was a sales rep for a packaging company. The purpose of the meeting was to explore ways he could be involved in our open house and gain from the exposure to the local businesses we'd have in. In return, ideally, we'd ask him to underwrite some of the costs. Simple enough.

The meeting was thoroughly enjoyable, but ultimately, we jointly determined that for this particular event, there wasn't a good fit for our organizations. That's when I was impressed.

Randy's entire focus was, "Well, how can I help you, anyway?"

The fact that he wouldn't get an immediate benefit was of less concern to him than building a relationship. It was backed up by his referring several folks to us.

Is the predilection to help others the result of Nature or Nurture? Is it something that is inherent in our genetic makeup? Or, is it a result of how we are raised? Our schooling? Our religious upbringing?

I am not a space cadet or cosmic dreamer. I am not given to religious proselytizing. Yet, I have witnessed time and again the power of those willing to help others getting paid back in both kindness and tangible reward many times over.

I am a sales professional. I've defended against aspersions cast on our profession that salespeople are greedy and selfish. My experience is that even the busiest of successful reps are willing to help others. In fact, for many sales people, the knowledge their product or service helps others is a mentality far more beneficial than the dread of having stuff that needs to be sold.

How can I help?

ROC

Katrina's Back Deck
High Point, NC

There are three words I use to create the acronym ROC. Sometimes I'll pronounce it "rock," as in, "rock on!" Other times, I'll pronounce the letters themselves "ARRR-OHHH-SEEE. Often, I'll sign internal memos to the sales staff, "ROC," instead of a more traditional sign-off. So, what does it mean? Where does it come from? Why should you care?

I believe I coined the term in a late-night budget review session at the home of The Oliver Group's owner. In a down sales cycle, the pressure was always on to seek new ways to get it through to the salespeople that they had to improve sales. Most good businesspeople (owners) recognize that if sales are down for the company, then the commissioned sales reps are also hurting. It's a shared interest in improving the situation and, in my mind, not the time to kick good horses when they are down. They know they are down.

Nonetheless, when an owner is pouring over a balance sheet, looking at financials and sales projections, their mind is more than likely on *their* financial concerns (including their responsibility to others in the company, shareholders, etc.) Their first thought isn't necessarily on the individual rep.

I worked for a person who was often thinking about the reps and the staff ahead of herself. In fact, this mentality led to her blurting out that she wished the reps would think about her and the staff and the *responsibility* they had to bring in revenue. "R" stands for responsibility.

The fact is that in most companies it is the salespeople that have to bring in the bucks. While everyone is important to the overall process, attracting and retaining customers largely falls on Sales.' A company's ability to function is contingent on the reps doing their jobs to prescribed levels. Without sales, nothing happens.

The rep's responsibility to a company is vital to several areas. First, there is a need for every company to operate with adequate cash flow. In a word, there's a need for stability. Secondly, most companies seek to expand either operations or revenues, which requires both capital investment and money for everything from marketing to R&D. After stability, many companies seek growth. Lastly, and of utmost importance to your employer, companies seek to make money. Profits are the end game and they are not possible without salespeople owning their share of the responsibility.

A salesperson needs to be their own manager when it comes to responsibility. The implied or contractual agreement with your employer is only one aspect of the big R. You have a responsibility far more personal than that. You have a responsibility to finance your life.

Whether you're a single person living in closet-sized apartment, or a married person with a stay-at-home spouse and six kids in a large house, you have financial obligations. And your financial responsibility goes beyond meeting this month's bills.

Your personal financial responsibility should extend to being able to enjoy your life. Chances are, if you're a successful salesperson, you work hard. You should be able to play hard, too. You also need to have money for a rainy day. And the earlier in your life you start saving for retirement, the magic of compounding works for you. You should view not being a burden to your grown children or society in the future as a responsibility.

In the workplace, it is important to understand the extent of your responsibilities. Certainly, you are responsible for results. You may have the burden not only of making sales, but of being responsible for other aspects of the sales process, from front end marketing and prospecting to back end manufacturing and fulfillment.

You may be required to maintain certain profit margins on the sales you make. In some companies, failing to meet those margins means there are consequences for the rep, such as a cut to their commissions, because the defined responsibility was not met. Many corporations also rely on their sales force to be the "ears on the street," holding them responsible for informal customer research.

I've spoken with sales managers in fields ranging from equipment sales to the garment industry, from broadcasting to baked goods. They all share an observation about Sales Reps: it is an ongoing battle to consistently get timely reports as regularly assigned. Salespeople have a responsibility to their management to do what is mandated. The information requested is generally not superfluous and is being requested for a reason. By taking the job, you're agreeing to provide what is necessary. Here is why it's in your interest to do so:

Like you, your sales manager only has 24 hours in a day. How much of their time they dedicate to helping you is somewhat in their control. Don't piss them off because the time will come when they can be of assistance in putting money in your pocket. But, given a choice, they are likely to help the other rep who hasn't been childlike in "not turning in their homework on time."

Also, as a result of not doing required bureaucratic work, you get a reputation within your own company of being irresponsible. It leads to your co-workers, support staff, owners and managers wondering if you are irresponsible in your dealings with customers, too.

Many sales professionals enjoy extensive freedom in their comings and goings. What matters is getting the job done! The price we pay for that freedom is acceptance of responsibility. "R" is a major component of big sales.

I recently hired a new rep. In her final interview we were discussing her preferences for how she liked to interact with a sales manager. She had no interest in being micro-managed, which is a good fit for my style of management. I have neither the desire nor the time to micromanage any of our sales staff.

Part of the discussion went into the kind of money she needed and desired in the future. It was clear she understood the potential of sales when she said, "What you offer is an opportunity. Not a guarantee. If I wanted a guarantee I'd get a job, make a salary, get a 3% raise each year and go home after my 40 hours. I want to control my upside." "O" is for *opportunity*.

The opportunity becomes realized as your sales and your commissions grow. You have the opportunity to control your financial destiny. You give yourself raises. You don't punch a clock.

If your company is sold and you were providing the revenue, the chance of new ownership wanting to retain your services grows. If you are successful in your industry and events lead to your company disappearing, the chance of a former competitor becoming a future employer grows. If you establish great sales skills and ever find yourself in the job market, your chance of landing a great new position grows. Sales offers the opportunity for career security.

Think of the people who work with you. In fact, if you're in the same office as your support people, look at them. You have the opportunity to impact their lives, too. More money to the company means ownership can reinvest in its people and improve the quality and standard of the staff's livelihoods.

Or perhaps the dollars you bring in get re-invested by the owner into new products or services for you and other reps to sell. You have the opportunity to impact the company's growth.

There are certain words I listen for when talking with a prospective Sales Rep. Among them is a desire to work with or help people. Through the benefits of your product or service you can help your customers. In fact, the reason they are buying is because you've met a desire or a need they perceived. Sales gives you the opportunity to help people. Opportunity is a big part of big sales.

With all of that responsibility on your shoulders, how do you make the most of the opportunity? In a word, it takes *commitment*. "C" is for commitment. What is it you are asking yourself to commit to? What are others asking you to commit to?

Starting at the end, commit to getting results. There is a huge difference in saying "You will try to sell a certain amount and knowing that you *will* sell a certain amount. As long as your goals are not unrealistic, emphatically committing to achieving them greatly improves your odds. as opposed to saying, "I'll try." Commit to getting results.

Now, what are the steps towards achieving those desired results? No matter what industry you're in, you must give it your best shot. Commit to giving 100%! The cheerleader in me says give 110% but that's impossible. 100% is all anyone has. Keep it real. Give a 100% commitment.

The notion of committing 100% to your sales life is not to say ignore your personal life. Have a life. Work hard, play hard, do good things for friends, family and strangers. All work and no play make a salesperson boring, grumpy and over time, a turnoff to others. If you're committing to be a superhero, putting in hours from 5:00 AM to 10:00 PM and working weekends, make that happen within a very directed and defined timeframe. It shouldn't be that way forever!

You can, however, commit to keeping your personal life and sales life separate. All the requirements of parenthood, spouse-hood, caring for aging parents or just caring for your home and cars interfere with sales productivity. Commit to managing those responsibilities and not becoming a slave to them.

Part of your commitment should be to maintain a well-rounded life. Protect your good name in both your personal and professional dealings. Maintain your health. Without it, you'll never achieve the same potential.

Commit to maintaining a full pipeline of sales activity. While ultimately the prospects have a say in your results, you control your time and what you do with it. Fill it up with customers. Some sales jobs are better achieved by focusing on the steps along the path as opposed to only looking at the end of the path. A full pipeline needs to be your commitment to yourself because without it big sales will never be attained.

What is the commitment you make to your customers? You represent a company and its products or services. Be sure you are comfortable with what you profess because the primary impression the customer has of you comes from what you say. And their impression of you is paramount in their buying decision. Commit to excellent customer service. Besides, it's the best prescription for repeat customers.

Your commitment to a position means you are committing to continual learning required to be an expert in your product, your competition and your industry. Your commitment includes learning from mistakes. Making them is okay. Making the same one twice is stupid and harmful to your income.

A sign of a true sales professional can be viewed in their commitment to the task at hand. "C" is a big part of big sales.

ROC, learn it and live it!

The Best Salesperson I Ever Met

Lobby of The Oliver Group
Greenville, South Carolina

O kay, for this chapter I may be exaggerating a little. It is possible that in over thirty-five professional years I've met better salespeople than the one I'm going to tell you about. Also, the fact that I'm calling a 4'x6' tile inset in the carpet of our old showroom a "lobby" is really stretching the concept.

While our main headquarters was a freestanding building, our other locations were mostly showrooms and sales offices set into office parks. We had 'No Soliciting' signs on our doors. Sometimes when we had a slow month I saw those signs and feared our own reps may have gotten confused and thought they were aimed at them.

One day, a girl walked into the office. She was about 15 years of age. Already that day we had been attacked by two different salespeople callously disregarding the "No Soliciting" sign – one that was trying to sell phone service and another pushing temporary personnel. The young girl was strike three.

She was carrying a nondescript brown box. What it contained was a mystery. Why she was there was also a question. Usually school-aged kids peddling goodies for booster clubs or church projects go door-to-door in residential neighborhoods, not in office parks.

As opposed to ignoring the sign about solicitation, she confronted it (unlike her adult predecessors that day). First, she apologized, "Sir, I'm sorry if this is soliciting. I'm not sure of the full extent of the meaning of the word so I don't know if it applies to me?"

From the standpoint of sales techniques, within her first fifteen seconds she had already accomplished three things:

1) She got her prospect talking
2) She made her prospect feel guilty (is the big, bad businessman really going to throw the adorable child out on her butt?)
3) She effectively asked for help, which is a great appeal to a prospect's humanity ("will the wise old adult explain the meaning of this funny word to me?")

My response was something to the effect of, "If you're here asking us to do anything or buy anything, then you're soliciting." Whether she was sincere or just incredibly well-trained, she responded, "Well, actually I'm just kind of the workhorse. I'm not asking for anything. It's my school that asked us to go around and look for people who would benefit from these products."

Not only was she selling stuff for a booster for her softball team, she was throwing a solid "pitch." Nobody ever wants to buy anything. But give me a chance to benefit from something and now you have my attention. – and, I would soon come to learn my money!

Also keep in mind the brilliance of this salesperson's territory-management skills. Her teammates were knocking their brains out going door-to-door, tripping over each other in the same few subdivisions. Whereas this budding Willie Loman decided if she could knock on one door with numerous prospects behind it, her success would be greater and her efficiency quota far superior to that of the other "reps."

"So, how does your school want me to benefit?" I asked. "Here's the thing," she replied. "Valentine's Day is "like" around the corner, and a lot of busy working people don't have time to get out and buy presents for their wives or girlfriends. Like, some rush out at the last minute to take care of "like" one special person, but they forget the other important people. Like their mothers or their secretaries..."

Sales Technique Review #2. The time elapsed from the intrusion was still under sixty seconds at this point and she had already:

4) Demonstrated empathy and understanding.
5) Conveyed a deep understanding of her prospect's needs.
6) Managed to hone in on her prospect's pain.

This fish was now nibbling at her hook! "Okay," I said. "I only have a minute or two to spare, show me what you have." My mistake, the sales ace was not ready to reveal her product line. First, she felt a detailed "discovery process" was in order. She asked, "Well, do you want to start with your wife or your mother?" "My wife." "Okay, when is the last time you surprised her with a little gift for no reason at all?"

At this point I was convinced I'd wind up either in hell or divorce court if I didn't quickly purchase from this cherubic huckster. "What sort of price range were you thinking would make a nice gift for your wife? What's her name, by the way?"

Sales Technique Review #3. About three minutes had passed:

7) A needs-ascertainment process was implemented.
8) "Your wife or your mother" didn't allow for an answer of "yes or no" regarding whether I'd buy – instead, it was a question of which I'd buy first.
9) The relative value of the purchase was established.
10) The prospect was asked to self-qualify their financial playing field.
11) She humanized the process – i.e. "your lovely wife Ellen, the mother of your children, the one who puts up with you..."

She opened the magic box of product offerings. She didn't ask, "Would Ellen like this?" She asked, "Which of these do you feel would be most appreciated by Ellen?" Now, we had a problem. There was mostly junk.

This buyer didn't like the salesperson's "solution" to making my wife feel special. I sought to end our brief sales encounter.

This kid wasn't taking no for an answer. "Okay," she said, "If you don't want to buy something for Ellen, how about even a small token of appreciation to someone on your staff or don't forget, we still need to talk about saying thanks to your mother..."

Sales Technique Review #4: Graduate School at the University of the 15-Year-Old Pushy One!

12) The assumptive close was evident - something would be purchased here.
13) Asking which would be "most" appreciated was like asking, "Which of these widgets will best expedite your manufacturing?" It's stating we have a variety of benefits to offer you and you have to consider all of them in order to come up with your ranking.
14) The product offered didn't meet the buyers need, so new needs were ascertained.
15) If you can't appeal to "fear" (you better make that wife of yours feel special), appeal to "greed" (you love it when mommy feels proud and don't you want to be the "thoughtful one" in the office?).

There was nothing I wanted to buy for anyone. What I wanted was to return to my office and not be attacked by the junior high girls' softball team for refusing to be a patron. Somehow, she read my mind! "Do you find my being here or my persistence annoying?"

Talk about a wake-up call. I was now wondering how I could recruit her to sell displays instead of finishing the 9th grade.

She continued, "I understand there may not be "Like" a "product" that you like, but..." And then there was silence. Either I had to kick her out or buy something. I asked, "Well, does it help you out if I just get one thing? And can we do it quickly?" At the speed of light, her cash bag and order pad were in hand. She helped me select some junk, then added, "This is the stuff we like, usually sell on a card table outside the supermarket. For Valentine's Day most men are a little behind..."

Final Sales Techniques as Demonstrated by the Teenage Master:

16) Understand what will alleviate tension in the process (she showed me a way out – just buy).
17) She played a bluff by asking a grown man to call a kid – other than one of his own – "annoying."
18) After learning I was a sales manager, she asked how I felt about persistence.
19) She got my attention back when it slipped away.
20) She used silence. He who talks first loses. I spoke.
21) She made the transaction easy.
22) She went for the upgrades.

I purchased a smelly bag of dried potpourri which sat in our cabinet for years. I brought it home that night thinking I'd be a romantic hero (Valentine's Day was still a month off). "Honey, look what I bought from a nice little girl today to make you happy." Ellen looked at me funny and just asked, "Why?"

Felix Unger Said It Best

"The Odd Couple" Apartment
Manhattan

Initially debuting as a stage play penned by Neil Simon, *The Odd Couple* next caught fans' attention in a 1968 movie version. Two years later, Felix and Oscar became a weekly staple in many living rooms for a five-year prime time television run. CBS then did a remake with Matthew Perry starring from 2015-2017.

Felix was the neat, finicky divorcee who shows up on the doorstep of Oscar Madison. Oscar, also divorced, was a sloppy sportswriter more attuned to watching the New York Rangers than seeing La Boheme at the Opera.

In one famous scene, Felix was berating Oscar for a characteristic goof. Oscar's excuse began, "I assumed…" Felix grabbed chalk and wrote in overly-large letters on the nearby blackboard: ASSUME. Emphatic in his denunciation of his roommate's excuse, Felix bellowed, "You assumed? When you assume you make an ASS (he circled the first three letters on the board) of you (he circles the "U") and ME (he circles the last two letters)!"

As salespeople, making assumptions can be deadly to our pocketbooks. Exceptions to this rule are limited to making certain allowances when you are ballparking pricing or very deliberately employing an assumptive closing technique. Otherwise, do not assume – do ask or clarify.

Here are some of the more common assumptions salespeople unfortunately make:

The person you are dealing with has decision-making authority.

At Group W, we developed a nationwide Teacher Recognition campaign that we were going to syndicate to TV Stations. A very major piece of the puzzle was getting the sponsor on board. The executives on our staff responsible for that had lined up Apple Computer as a potential sponsor.

We held several meetings with small groups from Apple's Education Division. Most were organized or coordinated by one particular person who had been the primary contact. A very quiet woman was present in the first two meetings and we were introduced to her as "Ann," who would be helping with the project. Ultimately, Ann turned out to be the senior-most Apple executive directly involved in the project. We had collectively assumed she was an assistant.

That price is the ultimate decision criteria.

I hate when a salesperson starts talking about price before the need, desire or benefits of a product are established. I've been on the receiving end of this approach from reps selling lawn service to me in my home, computer integration services in our business and vacation packages for my leisure. In other words, it's a pervasive mistake!

Does price matter? Does a client's budget need to be considered? Does a client's ability to fund the acquisition of a service or product matter? Of course! But should a sales rep be focused solely on pricing guidelines? Probably not.

I met with a client many years ago needing a tradeshow display. They made heating elements for electrical dryers. They said their budget was $2000. After digging, I learned their budget was based on what the owner's neighbor had paid for a display. I also learned their focus on price was a function of the owner knowing his neighbor was unhappy with the results of what he had bought, so my client was making sure he didn't overspend.

By not allowing these issues to overly influence my decision nor allowing them to lead me to falsely assume price was the overriding issue, I conducted a thorough discovery and found they were targeting large companies with enormous potential. Initially, they spent about $9000 with us. The client is still with us today, hundreds of thousands of dollars later – because we didn't assume.

That a customer hears what you say.

In the course of selling a product or service there are numerous interactions. Some will focus on the benefits and some will focus on the features. Some may be very detail-oriented and technical. Others may be extremely important but could be applied to almost any transaction. Examples of this last type might include issues such as quantity, delivery dates, training, shipping, etc...

Reps get into trouble when they assume a client realizes that the special incentive offered with the higher price options are not included with the budget offerings. Reps get into trouble when in the midst of focusing on six different details they mention a seventh item and assume the client has heard them.

Avoid trouble! Assume nothing. Everything that is part of your agreement should be in writing and be reviewed. Everything that was discovered in the needs-ascertainment process of your sales campaign should be documented back to the client in a discovery agreement.

That no news is good news.

It has happened on more than one occasion that a salesperson on our staff will learn one of their clients has just purchased from the competition. I'll ask, "Do we know why they bought elsewhere? And more importantly, why didn't we at least have the opportunity to bid on the project?"

There are two types of answers that are infuriating. First, "Well, *now* they say they really didn't like what they bought from us last time." Or, "They say there were always problems with the display. Why didn't they just call me?" These are signals that the rep's approach to that client was "no news is good news."

In those instances, the rep's failure had nothing to do with not making the new sale. It had everything to do with the rep assuming their client was a happy camper, instead of proactively maintaining contact and managing the account. No news isn't good news. It's a clear signal you aren't doing your job. Do not assume your clients are happy until they tell you they are happy.

That a prospect knows all about you.

Perhaps you work for the world famous Widgets America Corporation. You're meeting with the new purchasing agent at BuyerofWidgets.Com – the fastest growing on-line channel supplier for corporate widget buyers everywhere. Your company has been the leader in the industry for over 100 years. However, this dot.com is all of eight months old and rather than being staffed by industry veterans, most of the staff is under twenty-six and they know far more about e-commerce than they do about widgets.

As the widget seller, you can greatly hurt your chances of capturing this market if you assume the buyer knows about your products. Now, let's look at a more traditional example.

What if the company you were meeting with relied on widgets as an integral component of the machinery they produced? And what if they always bought from Widgets America Corporation?

Things are "happening" for this manufacturer. There is a new generation of management in charge. Everything is up for review. You, however, as the well-entrenched widget provider, take for granted that your place in their manufacturing process is secure. You fail to explain how the finely-tuned widgets you produce are custom calibrated for their needs. You don't address your years of above-average service that enabled them never to have a downtime in their production.

Meanwhile, a hungry competitor of yours has promised these items, beaten your price, and focused the new buyer's attention on service. They offered nothing you weren't already doing and the price they put forth was unrealistic. But for the first time in fifty years this client was now going to give this other company a shot, all because you *assumed* the new buyer knew all of this. Don't just educate a prospect on your benefits. Re-educate a client as to how you meet and exceed their needs or expectations.

That someone knows how to buy from you.

It should go without saying that a good sales rep will inquire about a prospect's prior experience with purchasing similar products. What we sometimes forget is that inexperienced purchasers may not know what to ask us, may not know all the things they should consider and may not know "how" to buy.

The question of "how" could be a function of financing: does the purchase come from a capital budget in one lump sum or can the same items be purchased via a leasing program that may come from an operational budget?

The same kinds of issues affect salespeople selling directly to consumers. The majority of homeowners buying underground sprinklers have not previously purchased one. Which is more important, the quality of the sprinkler heads, the pipes running between them, or the pressure of the hoses?

Here, the smart salesperson ascertains what the homeowner knows, as well as what they care about (i.e. having it installed before the in-laws get to town). Most importantly, they do not assume the buyer understands their materials will last twice as long as the less expensive competitors.

Assume nothing. Don't get hosed!

How Wiping My Butt
Saved A Client $5000

Knoxville Marriott
Knoxville, TN

T oo many volumes have been written solely dedicated to the topic of negotiating for me to attempt to do it justice in a small chapter. But a book about big sales needs to acknowledge the importance of negotiation and negotiating techniques. After all, theory aside, this book deals with reality.

Negotiation is rarely a pure form. It is tainted by circumstance, third parties, the laws of supply and demand, as well as the most unscientific of all creatures – humans and their egos.

I walked into WHAS-TV in Louisville, KY. The purpose of the meeting was to negotiate the renewal of *PM Magazine,* a half-hour long, nationally syndicated program that meant a lot to me. The program originated on the Westinghouse stations and then Group W syndicated it. When it started its run, I was in college and interning at the CBS Affiliate in Syracuse which carried the program. I was there at its inception, and over a decade later, I was there when Group W pulled the plug.

In my sales career I've been met by people glad to see me and I've been greeted by folks who'd just assume I wasn't about to waste their time. But never before had I been greeted at gunpoint!

I walked into the General Manager's office with a briefcase in my left hand and an outstretched right arm ready to shake his hand. His oversized desk chair was turned so he had his back to me, and all that was visible was the back of his head. Slowly, the chair turned, and my client was grinning as he pointed an AK 47 assault rifle at me.

"So, you want to talk about renewing your program and upping the license fee?" At that moment, one could say he had the upper hand in our negotiation. Thankfully, he wasn't a psycho – just a responsible manager who was holding the gun for his news department (so they wouldn't play with it). The station's news department was doing a story on assault rifles later that day. Ironically, months later this same station was the scene of an assault and murder involving gunfire.

Most dictionary definitions of "negotiate" include a reference to either *agreement* or *getting it done* (i.e. successfully negotiated the curve). Unless sales are successfully negotiated, they remain either "potential sales" or unprofitable ones.

Myth #1 is that a client wanting to negotiate is a bad thing – the truth is, if they weren't interested in successfully concluding an agreement to acquire your services, they probably have something better to do with their time than negotiate with you. So, welcome negotiation as the strongest of all possible buying signs. Most of the time, it's the same as the prospect saying, "I see some degree of value in what you offer and seek to establish terms I can live with to attain the value you offer."

Myth #2 is that negotiating and discounting are the same thing. Negotiating is a process of give and take, of striving for clarification of any issues, and of mutually giving up a little with the common goal of getting a deal done. Discounting means the seller provides the goods at less than the originally stated value.

Discounts take on forms other than just reducing the price. They may mean offering additional products or services at no charge. They may mean discounting the time value of money by stretching payments or reducing finance charges. In the same manner these elements can be discounted, so too can they be negotiated. So before acquiescing to your buyer's request, see what they are offering in exchange for agreement.

The key is to seek what is important to the party you are negotiating with. For instance, let's say I have a prospect who needs to buy an exhibit for a trade show that is at the end of August, but they have a fiscal year that starts September 1st. If I'm meeting with them about the sale sometime in June, they may be saying they love the display but can't buy it because there is nothing left in their budget.

If my knee-jerk response was to say, "let's make it x-thousand dollars less," all I've done is discount the value of my product and still not made a sale. However, by going through a process to isolate the objections (i.e. funds available), I can instead negotiate to successfully make a sale.

I have a product they want, need and have no qualms about. It is in their interest to successfully conclude a deal. What they need out of the negotiation is first, the product, and second, a way to pay for it in the following fiscal year. There are numerous ways I can solve that financing issue. Instead of offering a discount (and perhaps still not reaching an agreement), I can negotiate payment terms that meet their needs while also garnering the customer's goodwill.

'Half' Myth #3 is that the only successful negotiation is when both parties are satisfied and neither has taken advantage of the other. I call this a "half myth" because leaving the other guy with cab fare home instead of trouncing them is really just a good long term, self-serving business strategy. When selling is a career, you have an interest in allowing your customer to remain healthy and vibrant so they can be a repeat customer. And you don't want a customer saying anything negative about your negotiation methods. Word gets around and your reputation is your meal ticket.

Negotiation involves many considerations, not just price. In addition to what gets negotiated, reps need to be careful when to negotiate. If it's possible to suggest a universal answer, I'd suggest not negotiating until there is a decision on the prospect's part to acquire the product or service.

If you start negotiations too soon, you run the risk of not having fully conveyed the value of your product or service. Also, there is the risk of appearing desperate, which may plant doubts in a buyer's mind.

The biggest danger in negotiating is sending a signal that your price is flexible, your terms are not firm, or you have a lot more to add to the deal than you are being forthcoming about. Be careful when presenting your product and service that the prospect recognizes for each potential enhancement you mention, there is a commensurate additional expense.

Myth #4 is compromising. If you say the cost for an item is $10.00 and your customer offers $5.00, your compromise of $7.50 is not really a compromise. You are steadfastly agreeing to a deal. At the heart of negotiation is reaching agreement on terms you and the customer find acceptable and in both your best interests.

Sometimes it is not in your best interest to conclude a deal. Will the required level of servicing an account be a money loser or time killer? Will a price concession lead to a market-wide devaluation of your product? On the other hand, if you walk away from the prospect and refuse their low-margin offer, can you still hit quota or make payroll next month?

While a great negotiation tactic is to fully understand the implications of walking on a deal, a better one is having options. Enter a negotiation knowing what alternatives you have if the negotiation doesn't work out (ah, the luxury of a full sales pipeline). As a technique, be prepared to ask your prospect what their plan B is. A reminder that they need your stuff will enhance its value if the need is truly there.

Conversely, many sales fall apart because a prospect has an acceptable "Plan B." By learning what it is and familiarizing yourself with their preferences, you can impact your negotiating strategy. Perhaps if they can legitimately buy across the street it's not the time to play hardball. After all, results matter.

Years ago, one of our reps shared a phrase with me. I don't think he coined it, but I've used it many times since. He said, "Make the rules or break the rules." While we use this dictum in our design strategy for exhibit sales, it also applies to a negotiating strategy. Simply put, if your customer is focused on price, explore other areas that can be negotiated. Most of all, don't allow a competitor to set the terms under which you'll negotiate.

If the client is focused on an initial purchasing cost, change their thinking to one of "total cost of ownership." If the client is primarily focused on service – perhaps because they've had an inferior product in the past – then you may win by focusing on product quality. *You must address what they care about,* but you lose if their narrow scope of vision is focused on an area where you don't have a competitive advantage.

And sometimes, the most bizarre of real-world events can alter a negotiation. I had been in Atlanta to sell one of our TV Station image campaigns. We had a right of first refusal clause in place with one of the stations that gave them the chance to buy the successor campaign to the one we were presently providing to them. The product introduction went great and the terms started getting worked through.

They wanted to retain some elements of the old on-air campaign and not necessarily buy all of the new, but they understood if they didn't buy the new campaign that we'd sell it to a competitor. They wanted the new programming elements but to retain the rights to the old theme.

There was confidence all around a deal would ultimately get done. Most elements were in place, but the final dollars needed to be agreed to. I had to drive several hours up into Tennessee for meetings. We agreed to reconvene by phone the next day.

From my hotel in Knoxville we traded calls back and forth. I believe they were offering $125,000 and I was trying to get them to $138,000. The old package of program elements had zero value in that market to us. With each item I conceded to allow them to retain, the price climbed closer to my target. Unfortunately, I'm lactose intolerant.

When I eat something I shouldn't, my stomach violently reacts. I need a toilet, pills or both – quickly. Between the negotiations back in Atlanta, my meetings in Knoxville, and other calls in between, I never grabbed lunch, so once back in the hotel, room service brought me something. The something must have included cheese that I didn't notice, and my calls were now regularly being interrupted by urgent trips to the bathroom.

It was in one of these abbreviated conversations that the Atlanta station said they'd be calling back in five minutes with their final offer because we were already over their budget. At that moment in time, I was far more interested in the comfort of the golden throne then I was in their offer. But, expecting the call back, I hurried to do my business (lactose intolerance is not an exact science).

The phone rang while I was still occupied. But I knew who was calling, why they were calling and adding a hundred thirty thousand something dollars to our sales was of interest! Alone in the hotel room I waddled to the phone (pants at ankles, very attractive). They offered $133,000 and I took it with the only stipulation being that they made the call shorter than thirty seconds so I could go wipe my ass.

You just never know what will affect big sales!.

What's Your Hourly Rate?

Katrina's Doctor
High Point, NC

W hen my accountant works on taxes for us, we get billed by the hour. For the associates to work on our returns or planning it costs us about $100 an hour. For the partners to review it I believe the bill is about $300 an hour.

I used to joke with my brother the lawyer and ask him if when we spoke during the workday his "meter" was running. Many law firms and other professional practices will break down time increments for billing purposes into *twelfths* of an hour.

We just had our lawnmower repaired and there was a sign in Hap's Engine Shop indicating the labor fee. Another sign said, "If you want it *now* the labor fee jumps to $75/hr." When the flush valve on the urinal in one of our showrooms needed replacement, that was $65/hour for labor.

I was very happy when Craig, our teenage son, was working at a day camp getting an hourly wage one summer. But he liked it more when he would cut someone's lawn and get two or three times his camp hourly wage for the same timeframe.

With the exception of retail and some telemarketing/inside sales positions, most sales professionals are not concerned with an hourly wage. However, more should be. Here's why:

The sooner you can recognize an inefficiency in your sales activity the greater the likelihood you can adjust before it becomes pervasive and counterproductive. If you know that based on goals, quotas and/or personal financial need you should sell x amount per hour and you realize you've already put many hours into something that only has a value a fraction of x, then something is wrong.

If meeting the required x seems forever elusive, perhaps it's a sign that there is an inherent problem with either the product, the process, the presentation or the presenter. Using a time frame allows you to better measure the efficiency and results of differing initiatives.

For many reps, there is an instant elevation in self-esteem and their sense of being a professional when their "hourly rate" turns out as high as many of the doctors and lawyers. Sometimes to get there, we'll look not at what the rep puts in their pocket each hour, but at what they need to be generating for their company. Your lawyer and accountant work the same way. Those two, three and four hundred dollar per hour billing rates go to their firms, not all in their pockets!

So here is how you calculate your hourly rate:

Start with your annual quota or goal. It's either been assigned to you or you've settled on a number based on how much you ultimately want to earn in a year. (For instance, if you make 15% commission on gross sales and want to earn $75,000 than you have to sell $500,000 worth of product).

Divide your target sales number ($500,000) by 2,000 hours. 2,000 hours equates to fifty weeks at forty hours per week. We'll presume that two weeks a year are for vacation. You may have to adjust your calculations by your work and vacation habits. In this simple example, the reps hourly billing rate is $250. That's entering partner territory at many law and accounting firms.

Sales Managers and small business owners should use this method with their staffs as a way of further demonstrating a sales person's responsibility to their company. No position other than sales more directly brings in the revenue that is the lifeblood of an organization.

Reps will need to use their new hourly rates as a guide and not necessarily as a strict, exact, 'to-the-second' accounting of how their time is being spent. Too close an adherence to an hourly rate can also be dangerous. It may lead to showing impatience to clients and thus chasing away prospects. Focusing solely on a time/value equation could potentially also lead to your not investing in the development of a potential prospect because their initial order may be small, despite that client's value over the life of the relationship.

Knowing the value of your time is critically important for salespeople. Getting others to value it is at times a challenge. In fact, if you don't zealously guard against wasting it or allowing others to waste it, who will?

I bought my company from Katrina, whose late husband had founded The Oliver Group. Katrina is a very successful apparel designer and owner of the self-named manufacturing firm that sells lingerie and sleepwear in high-end boutiques around the world.

One day, Katrina had an appointment with a doctor. She, along with many other patients was kept waiting well beyond a reasonable time. She vowed if the doctors kept her waiting again on her next follow-up visit, she'd bill them for her time. Sure enough, at the next appointment the waiting room was again full and the wait time quite lengthy.

Apparently, the doctor's reception staff was used to the complaints and immune to their employer's greed for cramming too many patients into too little time. Katrina did have her office bill the doctor for her time. While I don't believe it was ever paid, I wish I could have been a fly on the wall to see the bill opened.

What's your time worth?

What's In A Name?

LD Momar Associates
West Palm Beach, Florida

If there were such a thing as a guard gate to enter the world of sales, nobody would be allowed to pass through until they demonstrated a thorough understanding of the power of "referrals." Unfortunately, many salespeople I meet are well-aware of how important a referral can be, but do not actively cultivate them.

Getting others to talk about you can be the kiss of death if they aren't saying good things. Let's say one of your customers is angry at you. Their shipment was late, and it was incorrect. The parts of what they ordered that were right were damaged. And as a result of your company's poor delivery, lousy production, and messed up fulfillment, your customer is now in a big-time predicament with their own clients or manufacturing processes.

Now, let's say the owner of the company your firm has just damaged goes to a local business function or industry gathering that evening, when his or her blood is still boiling. Every innocent "how ya doing" or "what's new" leads to a rant about how your company screwed them. It's not necessarily that they were out to badmouth you. They were just talking about their bad day.

Now, the thirty people the owner spoke with at the party have a picture of your company in their heads. It's a big warning sign that says, "Be careful doing business with these guys because they don't get the orders right, they ship out damaged products, and they are always late." Over the next week or so, all thirty of those people find an opportunity to share your story with other colleagues, friends, relatives or strangers.

As the business version of the game of "telephone" plays out, the facts become obscured. What started as a simple shipping and paperwork error and perhaps a minor flaw in a tiny section of product that went undetected in your otherwise diligent quality assurance process has now turned into someone saying, "They make crappy products and don't give a damn about their customers!"

The strength of your good name is only overshadowed by the speed with which it diminishes when your reputation gets sullied.

Look at the same scenario if you sell services. I remember meeting with a client that provided both plant maintenance and industrial security services. The security portion of their business was taking off because a major competitor had developed a bad reputation for the personnel it hired. Apparently, many of its Security Officers were ex-cons willing to work for the extremely low wages and no benefits in exchange for being given a quasi-cop uniform and "access" to other people's businesses.

There are industries that rely heavily on referrals. Real estate salespeople go to great lengths to attract referrals for listings. Automotive salespeople don't just want you to come in and visit the Toyota dealer. They want that person who just drove off the lot in a new Camry to send their friends *specifically* to see Dave at the Toyota place.

Some years back, when Ellen and I met with a financial planner from Prudential Investments, we needed help from someone who was far better versed in money management than we to help us prepare for our kids' education and our retirements. Going into the meeting, however, I was skeptical that they'd kill us with fees for transactions or charge a huge retainer.

To our delight, the "fee" for their advice was to provide the names of three people we knew that he could call and use our name as an introduction. It was a systematic way of gaining referrals.

More recently, a group of five families with whom we're friends vacationed together in Orlando. While there, one of the families purchased a time-share. This led to a great celebration by one of the other families as they had originally referred the time-share salespeople to our friends who bought. As a thank you, they would receive a bonus of 40,000 Marriott Rewards points. Timeshare salespeople formally cultivate referrals. Do you?

I recently met with a new contact from the corporate headquarters of a nationwide restaurant company. Following our initial discovery meeting, I presented a solution that would meet her needs. The area of the company she is involved with is "supplier diversity," which essentially means that as a big company, they try to do as much business as possible with companies owned by minorities or women.

She told me that she had been pitched many times by display companies who were minority or women-owned but never had the need for a display. Now, when she did have the need, she had talked with their marketing, human resource and franchise development departments, all of whom had bought displays, and all of whom had bought them from me. Based on their comments about our products and services, she had decided to work with me, despite the fact she might get flak from coworkers saying she should buy from a *registered* minority or woman-owned firm.

Because of the recommendations I had been given, she also felt safe recommending me to a friend in a similar position at another huge international company with a regional headquarters in our area.

Those original referrals became even more valuable. Although my contacts at these companies didn't know it when we first met, at that time a woman actually did own our company. My new clients have told me that there is a whole network of diversity supplier executives they'll be introducing me to. What is it your clients will be saying about you?

Prior to so much of our marketing moving on-line, one of the strongest marketing pieces our vendor supplier provided was a glossy newsletter/ brochure essentially made up of successful case studies. Clients share how they succeeded in their trade show marketing programs, were more efficient, got more leads, and had great presence at shows. Really, the marketing piece is a way of "bottling" referrals.

Sales people should have a method for capturing testimonials as well as a formal, ongoing referral program. After all, we all know it's great when we get a referral, so why not get them more often? Solicit social media endorsements and save e-mails that are share-worthy in the future.

Public Relations firms can play a role for a company in publicizing their good name and proactively putting forth good news stories of how a company's products and services benefit clients. Individual reps should develop their own PR campaigns. Some of the elements may include specific presence at networking events, press releases about major contracts, or arranging to be a speaker in front of audiences that you want to view you as a winner or leader.

Larry Momar, co-owner of a telemarketing service, sat in his Florida office and dialed my number in South Carolina. The first time he reached me, I was in the middle of putting out some fire and on the cell phone rushing somewhere. Normally, if a salesperson has the juice to track me down on my cell, they get points in my book for aggressiveness but it's not necessarily memorable. In this case, Barry acknowledged it wasn't a good time to talk, but indicated that he had been given my name by two sales managers at other Skyline Distributors because they felt I'd be interested in learning how he had helped them increase their business.

I was not looking to buy/contract with an outside telemarketing service. However, I'm always looking for ways to increase our business. Thus, I was open to speaking with him when he called back at the time he indicated he'd phone.

The key to our becoming a client of his lay in the initial use of saying he was referred to me by people whom I not only respect, but who understand the business I'm in because they are in it, too.

The power of a good name can open many doors and be a large component in your quest for big sales.

Is Prejudice Limiting
Your Income?

The King Center
Atlanta, GA

I 'll admit it. When it comes to a certain product, I am unabashedly prejudiced and will not buy. In fact, I'll go so far as to leave one store that may only have this product from members of my "bigot" class and go on to another store to find a similar product from the group I'm comfortable with. The product?

Fiction (spy novels, crime, legal thrillers) written by women or where women are the main characters. Worse than reading about how the killer applied their make-up is listening to it as an audio book. I cannot bring myself to listen to them if they are the audio book equivalent of "chick flicks."

By avoiding books written by or voiced by females, I'm relatively certain that I have missed out on some great stories. The problem is that every time I've tried to expand my horizons I either hate the story and never finish it, or fall asleep while driving down the road.

I have no other prejudice that I'm aware of – however, as a consumer, I'm sure I have biases, and as a business person, I'd be surprised if some unconscious episode in my past didn't occasionally play a role in my decision making. It is the price we pay for being human and the joy we celebrate for living a full life that has not been cloistered.

When it comes to selling, I can't afford to be prejudiced (or to pre-judge). Casting stereotypes onto prospects only creates barriers that may not be there.

One of our sales reps worked feverishly to close a deal with a company based in Hong Kong. The combination of language differences, time differences, and too many decision makers (or influencers) in the mix had the rep exasperated to the point where she exclaimed, "I don't ever want to do business with another Chinese company again."

I'm not a sociologist or historian and my numbers may be off, but I commented, "Gee, that's a shame. I'm sure a few of those billion people may at some point need a trade show display." You can't let one bad experience limit your future dealings, but as with all experiences, you can dig deep for lessons to be learned.

Ironically, two days later, she phoned to say she had closed a (smaller) deal with another Chinese company that had an office in the Carolinas!

You can't judge a book by its cover. One of our salespeople told a story at a sales meeting many years ago of how she had sold a sizable display project to a company that makes swimming pools. The rep had been asked to come to the pool company's office. The office was in a "slum." The rep barely felt safe leaving her car and walking the half block to the building.

The pool company had a tiny sign and their office was in the basement. Many companies in the business world go to great lengths to create a work environment where the décor makes a great first impression. This was not such a company. The discovery meeting went well, but the rep was very skeptical that a company that didn't care how it looked would spend the kind of money needed to create the kind of display the discovery process called for. They did buy – and they upped the ante with several add-ons.

It didn't matter what their office looked like. They called on clients at their homes or on wholesale client retailers who carried swimming pools. However, when they were in front of clients that did matter (at trade shows), that was when they wanted to look good, so they bought a nice exhibit. The point is, had the rep followed her hunch that an office in a slum meant no money and no chance of a deal, she'd have lost out on thousands in commission.

I feel lucky that one of my first bosses when I left college was a woman. It showed me from day one in business that gender didn't matter – or, at least, shouldn't matter. There remains a wage gap in the earning power of females vs. males in the U.S. We still have work to do – however, twenty years back I knew the tide was starting to turn for us as a society. I illustrated this in a riddle I shared with my kids and some of their friends:

When I was in elementary school, a women's lib advocate came to the school auditorium and told the story of a little boy who was riding in a car with his father and there was a horrible accident. The father was killed instantly. The boy, badly hurt, was taken by ambulance to the hospital and rushed into surgery. The surgeon approached the patient and declared, "I can't operate. This boy is my son." When she asked the audience to explain, "How that could be?" there were wild guesses, but none correct.

The same riddle told to a much smaller group of kids a generation later instead led to blank stares and comments like, "Gee, dad, you must have been stupid. That's easy, the surgeon was the boy's mother."

Many sales reps still fall victim to pre-judging a situation where they meet male and female prospects and automatically assume the male is in charge. The mistake can be compounded if the rep never seeks to clarify their initial assumption and spends the bulk of the meeting addressing the male and ignoring the female superior.

Beyond ethnic and gender stereotypes, I've seen people handicap their income due to their prejudice against homosexuals, religious groups, or race. It's not exactly breaking news that bias, stereotyping and prejudice exist and will likely continue to exist in some form or another for time eternal. And, if they exist in society, why wouldn't they exist in business?

If you choose to pursue big sales, you need to be open. If you prejudge a prospect based on your irrational fears, lack of familiarity or past experiences, you put limitations on yourself or your income.

A rep that worked for me was recapping his meeting with an executive and after all of the pertinent info was shared, he added, "Besides, I think he's a fella who's light in his loafers. My 'gaydar' is usually pretty accurate." In a subsequent discussion of the same account, the rep made another reference to the prospect's purported homosexuality.

I asked if he had any personal friends, relatives or acquaintances who were homosexual and he answered, "No." Then, he defensively added, "But I'm not prejudiced against them or anything." I asked if his awareness of the client's sexual preference was on his mind when he met with or spoke to him?

His answer was honest. Unfortunate, but honest. He indicated that whenever he was with the prospect, the topic was foremost on his mind and was "weirding him out." The prospect had not done anything inappropriate, nor was he flamboyant in dress or mannerisms. Yet, an otherwise logical, aggressive salesperson was not functioning in his normal zone because of discomfort, irrational fear, and ignorance. As a result, the prospect bought from another company.

I've worked for managers who happen to be homosexual. Perhaps the entertainment world was more tolerant about people being "out," but I'd like to think it just didn't matter! I've also had African American bosses and Hispanic bosses. Talent comes in all shapes, sizes, colors, religions and ethnicities. The minute we start pre-judging based on those characteristics, we miss the opportunity to surround ourselves with beneficial people.

I wonder how many of you make judgments based on societal stereotypes? Retail salespeople and business-to-consumer reps make snap judgments all the time based on surface appearances – from homes, cars and clothing to speech patterns and education.

You wouldn't want to sell to a guy who's got this wild concept for a big 'ol' general store in rural areas away from the big cities. I mean, this guy was wearing denim overalls and drove a dirty old pickup truck. How much could he buy? The fact that I just described Sam Walton may have been missed by some.

And hey, one thing we're sure of is that if the product is complicated we're not going to deal with any kind of college dropout – but that's a shame if you had avoided doing business with Microsoft in its early days.

I've also been witness to several people who've used ethnicity to their business benefit. There is a sales rep working for the Los Angeles Skyline Distributor who is making a killing calling on Korean companies in her territory. Good, bad, or otherwise, it appears many of those companies are more comfortable doing business with her as she, too, is Korean.

Much of marketing is reliant on demographic groups and media empires have been built on targeting certain minority groups.

The concept of women being a minority is numerically false in society at large and increasingly they have the same opportunities as men in the business world. Meanwhile, the combination of opportunity offered in a free country, the availability of capital, the inherent respect for a strong work ethic and a variety of laws continue to bring immigrants to our shores. For some, they represent the competition. For others, they increase the customer base.

There is only one color you should be concerned with. It is the green of money – more of which can be yours the more open you are to all people around you. To paraphrase Dr. Martin Luther King Jr. (and I mean no disrespect), "Do not judge a prospect by the color of their skin, but by the content of their ability to purchase!"

What You Don't Say Says A Lot!

A few blocks from the Champs Elysees
Paris, France

On a festive New Year's Eve, I was wandering the streets of Paris. Having just finished a semester abroad, I was spending several weeks traveling throughout Europe before returning to the States. Fireworks lit up the night sky and everywhere people seemed of good cheer.

I had met some people at a youth hostel where I was spending the night, and one of the guys and I took a walk to explore, to enjoy, and quite probably to drink. We were surprised at the level of allowable rowdiness that seemed to coexist with what at that time was seemingly tight security. But it was New Year's Eve!

Safety was not foremost on our minds as we drank in the city and its celebration. It's not that we got lost – we just didn't have a destination or any particular care at the time as to where we wound up. However, we apparently strayed too far from the tourist zone. We found ourselves surrounded by six guys wanting our money and particularly, my overcoat.

Already several years removed from my high school French class, my ability to understand their demands was limited, but the message was clear. Between the menacing looks, the pushing, and little things like switchblades and pipes in some of their hands, there wasn't much of a need for dialog.

Comically, I tried to utilize my limited French, and while being threatened by six thugs I sternly and proudly said "C'est mon vestments." Roughly translated, I was ranting, "It is my clothes. It is my clothes." Sometimes words don't work well and in retrospect my choice of action probably wasn't the smartest.

When words failed me, I punched the biggest guy in the face, grabbed another guy and rammed his head into the side of a car. Without saying a word, I communicated to them far more effectively than when I tried to use inadequate words. I saved my ass – and my overcoat. They ran off and I lived to write about it!

The lesson here is the incredible power and danger of non-verbal communication. Powerful, because both *how* and *what* you communicate impacts the manner in which you, as a salesperson, are perceived. Dangerous, because too much of the time, too few of us are conscious of all the messages we are sending.

As professional salespeople, we've been taught to be observant. We look for clues in the mannerisms, body language, preparedness and energy level shown by our prospects. We listen not only for words, but for tone of voice and inflection. So, what's good for the goose is good for the gander!

Your prospects and clients are also observing you. Is what you are communicating a planned message or an inadvertent impression you are creating? Let's take a look at some of the ways sales professionals communicate in a non-verbal manner.

When do you show up?

Being prompt is a rarity these days. The very act of being on time and/or a little early conveys that you value your prospect's time. The fact that you are legitimately running late may be excusable, but not alerting an appointment that you are running late is most decidedly a black mark against you.

Being too early for a sales call may also send a negative connotation. "Gee, if this sales rep is over thirty minutes early, they must not have too much of importance to do?" Or, "Don't they have other customers? Am I the only one foolish enough to agree to see this rep?" Even the slight chance of these thoughts entering a prospect's mind before you can open your mouth could be a sales killer.

How do you get there?

It may not be rational, but it's real. When a salesperson calls on me, if I happen to notice they are driving a new Mercedes, I wonder if they bought that car with inflated margins on their product.

Conversely, being a New Yorker, it's taken me many years to get used to a "white collar" professional driving a pickup truck. Living and working in the Carolinas, it is not uncommon. However, when I see a sales person emerge from a pick up prior to calling on me, I'm instantly starting to classify them as "blue collar," regardless of what they are selling. (Hey self: refer to chapter on prejudice!)

My point is not to confess to my own snobbishness, but to convey that virtually everyone has a bias for or against something. I've met people in Detroit that simply won't do business with anyone driving a foreign car because it's viewed as an assault on the local economy. The car you drive up in, if seen by a prospect, may begin to communicate for you long before you get to the front door.

What are you wearing?

The professional world is not as simple as it once was when it comes to clothing. Instead of "white collar" and "blue collar," we now have business attire, business casual, semi-formal, or uniformed dress codes.

Both men and women run the risk of hitting either extreme in the dress code challenge. If an office is business casual and a woman decides to wear a suit, is she seen as too "plain?" Is she "stuck up?" Is she interviewing and looking for a new job? If a man shows up in what he thought were appropriate khaki business slacks and others view them as dungarees, is he viewed as "a slob?" Is he cheap? Is he merely fashion-challenged?

The importance of clothing is that it is a big part of the first impression you make on a prospect. Do you want to be viewed as professional? Successful? Coordinated? Neat? On the cutting edge? Impressions can be tailor-made by what you choose to wear. And all add to how your important words will be perceived – when you finally get around to conversing.

What do you bring with you?

Are you the rep that has papers strewn about, awkwardly stuffed into loose files (or piles) that you haphazardly carry into meetings? Or, do you have neatly typed, color-coded file folders that in and of themselves shout to the prospect across the conference table, "I'm organized and care about your account?"

Have you prepared a presentation dossier specifically for the important meeting you are entering, or are you rifling through dog-eared brochures stuffed in the bottom of your briefcase to put your best foot forward?

What, if anything, are you conveying to the packed conference room if you show up with an easel style flip chart when your competition just left after wowing them with a custom video presentation? Conversely, if you are selling a product or service that isn't "high tech," does an electronic presentation send the message that your company wastes money on fancy gadgets and therefore your price is too high?

How do you track the information they share?

Some people have excellent memories. Very few people have memories as good as they think they are – they've just forgotten that fact.

Unless a salesperson shared a graduation certificate from a memory-training institute or presented medical evidence of total recall, I'd be offended if they didn't take notes in a meeting. Other than relationship building, if a sales person isn't in a meeting to learn about a prospect's needs or present a solution, there's probably something better they should be doing with their time. For either of those reasons, and even if it is just relationship building, notes are in order.

By not taking notes, or by not capturing an especially noteworthy piece of data shared by your prospect, you are creating an impression of either arrogance, ignorance, or indifference.

How are you sitting?

Hey slouch, sit up straight! No, it's not your mother at the dinner table. This is your "sales conscience" talking.

I have witnessed professional salespeople virtually recline to the point of looking asleep when they should be sitting upright, or even leaning in, to convey interest in what the prospect is saying. I have witnessed salespeople mistake a congenial atmosphere for an invitation to put their feet up on a prospect's desk.

Not only does good posture show respect, it helps you breathe better, thus keeping you more alert. But putting aside the physiological reasons – it's easy to understand that being a slouch speaks volumes before you open your mouth.

What's happening on the outside of your head?

SMILE!

People respond to smiles involuntarily. It physiologically relaxes your prospect and relieves tension. Both are positive steps towards setting a stage for them to be more receptive when you do speak.

If you smile and they look at you, will they see a clean face? Do you have any distinguishing facial characteristics that will distract? I'm not referring to uncontrollable beauty marks, scars or abnormalities. If they are present, I'm sure you are quite conscious from other areas of your life that people notice and may be either intrigued or taken aback. But there are plenty of controllable facial issues that affect how your prospects will perceive you.

Ladies, is the makeup you are wearing doing you justice or harm? Men, is the mustache that once added character to your weak lip now an out of control weed? And speaking of facial hair, be sure there isn't any growing where it shouldn't be!

What's happening on the top of your head?

Because our overall appearance impacts our prospect's expectations of us, our appearance matters. Because our prospect's opinion of us as people is the first of several major hurdles towards a sale's culmination, our appearance matters a lot.

Is the haircut you are sporting the same one you had fifteen years ago? Maybe that's good, maybe that's bad. I'd suggest getting opinions from others just to be sure you're not lying to yourself about its attractiveness.

Beyond style, the other important factor is the degree to which you maintain your grooming. Put simply, get a haircut and keep it neat! And depending on the industry in which you operate, visible tattoos and piercings may be fine for your company, but until you have that figured out, caution may be advisable.

What's happening on the inside of your head?

Do your eyes flicker about and wander? Do you lack the ability to look your prospect in the eye or divert your attention when they look at you? If so, you are creating mistrust.

Now you're meeting with a potential client. Is your head in the game? Is it even in the same room as your client and your meeting? In other words, are you paying attention and focused? Are you listening and are you hearing?

If the client feels you're not with them in the meeting, what is the likelihood they'll be with you for the long haul?

What are your extremities doing?

I've worked on certain sales campaigns that required one-man dog and pony shows. Those types of presentations (after due diligence) are more like performances than meetings. As part of my preparation, there have been times I've rehearsed a gesture such as slamming my hand on a conference table for emphasis or jumping out of my chair in excited animation.

These are examples of positively using hands and legs in a conscious manner during the sales process. Many salespeople would be sick if they saw video of themselves that captured the unconscious mannerisms we are all guilty of.

Do your fingers nervously thread through one another during a meeting? Does your foot tap or do your heels click? Do you "drum" on the underside of your chair? Does your index finger flick at your thumb cuticle? Do you turn, twist or play with rings on your fingers?

Are you creating a distraction? Are you sending a message to your prospect that they bore you, that you'd rather be elsewhere, or that you've lost patience with their concerns?

Message to Reps everywhere: don't let what you don't say get in the way of your big sales.

It's All Relative

Savannah River Site
Aiken, SC

W hat a moment! If only it had been true.

I was in Georgia, driving between Savannah and Macon. At the time, my employer was Westinghouse, parent company to Group W TV Sales' Target Marketing Group. We were launching a new project called "Time To Care," which was a packaged television station image and marketing campaign.

That day was a good one. My presentations went well, and I knew that more than one player in the market was interested in the project. In fact, I already had a more-than-adequate offer from one station to buy the program package.

As a Northerner, whenever I was in the South, adjusting to the more limited options on the radio dial was a frustration. Over time, I learned to love country music. Thankfully, years later as a Southern resident, if I'm in a car without satellite radio or Bluetooth, the radio dial seems to offer more choices than only country or religious programming. But on that day, it was a news update that caught my attention.

A year or so earlier, DuPont Corporation had notified the United States Department of Energy that it would not seek to renew its contract to operate the Savannah River Nuclear Complex. The news announced that Westinghouse had just signed an initial three-billion-dollar agreement to take over operation of the site.

I was relatively certain my boss knew I was in Savannah that day. The fact that the Savannah River Site was hundreds of miles away in a different state did not deter my mind racing to calculate my commission on a $3 billion sale! With the math complete I called my office and got the boss on the line.

I informed him that things had gone well in Savannah and asked if he had heard the news? I then informed him of my two sales that day. One was for about $30,000 for the "Time to Care" package. The other was for a three billion contract to manage a nuclear site!

When it comes to what you sell, it's all relative. Okay, this year you sold a million and that's up ten percent over last year. Great! But how is it compared to two or three years ago when you were selling a million and a half?

You've sold better than any month in your history with your company. Congratulations. Feel good and do whatever you do to pat yourself on the back. Now, put on your cynic's glasses and ask how it compares to other reps in your organization. How does it compare to your competition? How do your results compare to your goals? How do you stack up against salespeople with like-sized market territories?

Not enough relativity for you? Here's a true "relative" story about my father-in-law. He was a great guy in every way. He owned his own business and had owned and managed others in the past. Earlier in his career he worked for a large corporation. He happened to be the first person I spoke with when I finally had what at the time was my "breakthrough" sale of a trade show display.

My in-laws were visiting us in South Carolina. I had been with The Oliver Group selling Skyline for several months. It was long enough to have built up serious doubts about whether or not I could sell the stuff. And, coming off what I considered to be a disaster of working at Fox after "mutually agreeing" that I leave Pennsylvania, I really was in no mood for a failure.

Relative to other reps at Oliver, I started out well. However, relative to my personal financial needs and goals, it was not happening at an acceptable pace. Additionally, I was seriously running up my draw advance against future earnings. That was when the South Carolina Department of Public Safety came into my life.

The project was about sixteen thousand dollars. Even once the client agreed to buy, we had to play some funny games to get around the state's normal procurement procedures. I took my lead from the state police and figured they would never ask me to do something illegal. But acquiescing to their request to break up the invoice into four separate deals sure felt smarmy!

On the Friday afternoon of my in-laws' visit, I had made plans to leave work a little early to meet my father-in-law for a round of golf. I had been putting in seven days a week for a long time trying to build my pipeline, so I figured two hours off on a slow Friday wouldn't kill my career.

Pulling into the parking lot at the golf course, I got the call from the SC Department of Public Safety's purchasing office, confirming their order. I was ecstatic. I told Jim, my father-in-law, about the order and he was happy for me. But what stands out is that he said, "Sixteen thousand, that's a big order!"

The point is, beyond being happy for me, from a business standpoint, he was viewing a raw number without the benefit of how it compared to other sales of similar product. I remember thirty years ago hearing about a bond salesman friend of mine who had sold several million dollars' worth of municipal bonds. I thought it was a huge sale, and he was worried he'd be sacked for the small size of the order. We all come to numbers with a ton of baggage that forces a comparison to something.

How do your clients view your numbers? What do they compare it to?

Sometimes I'm reminded of the sheer madness of numbers when large public companies announce their earnings. For example, "Corporation X announced third quarter performance today including sales of 2.1 billion dollars, resulting in a net loss of $843 million." Now, compare that to the tiny company that during the same three months had sales of 92 thousand dollars and expenses of 58 thousand. The owner here is on track to have an annualized profit of $132,000 at the end of a year. Sure beats losing eight hundred million in three months – but it's only numbers. Keep them in perspective.

I have a friend who owns a textile business. Where the Carolinas were once the home for this industry, that home is now scattered between Pakistan, China, Mexico and other places offshore. Tens of thousands of workers have been let go for cheaper labor around the world. Over a hundred mills have shut down and entire cities have been decimated by the loss of textiles going overseas.

The nature of my friend's business has changed dramatically over the years. At one point, they manufactured a well-known household brand name of garments. When their ability to manufacture at a price point that the market would accept disappeared, they switched their operations to sewing and finishing piece goods that are manufactured off-shore.

The result of N.A.F.T.A. combined with cheap labor in the mid-east and far-east has choked off much of that business, too. I asked him recently how his business was doing. His reply was, "I could sell a lot and hire back many people – if I wanted to lose money on every job."

Both in sales and in business, it's not what you sell, but what you keep.

My parents had a friend who made jewelry on a ping-pong table set up in the basement of her home. She and her husband would make the rounds at craft shows, and they made a little money along the way. One day, she was in Manhattan and approaching Macy's at Herald Square when the idea struck her to phone the Macy's jewelry buyer in hopes of making a big sale.

She got an appointment, and the buyer was thrilled with the samples. So thrilled, in fact, she ordered *several hundred gross* of each design for their stores around the world. The ping pong table wasn't big enough. It was a great sale, but eventually worth zero as our favorite jewelry designer had to pass on the order. Without production and fulfillment capacity, the real order was nothing more than a pipedream. Ah, numbers. They are all relative!

What ultimately matters as a sales rep are those numbers that reflect you've generated ample sales to meet or exceed your financial goals. Ideally, along the way you have not only contributed to your company's stability, growth, and profits, but have assisted a customer in satisfying a need or achieving their stated goals.

Winning Olympic Gold
Or An Oscar

Hotel Ballroom
St. Paul, Minnesota

C lichés become clichés because they are repeated frequently, are simply true – or both. Jaded sales professionals (including some who may be reading this book) have been known to roll their eyes and shun advice when it is presented in a manner they've heard one hundred times before.

The knee-jerk reaction is, "Don't waste my time with that warmed-over saying." The result is that rather than heed the advice, the recipient sometimes rejects it. The message is overshadowed by the messenger's approach.

When it comes to your income, you do not want to lose the opportunity to be a winner. So when I tell you the art of salesmanship requires practice and rehearsal, much like those of athletes and actors, don't roll your eyes unless you've already won all of the competitions you plan on entering. Of course, as salespeople, we compete on almost every piece of business.

Even if you are selling something that is a slam-dunk piece of business where there is no overt competition, you are still "competing" with the customer's expected level of service, product performance and pricing. Know too that the smartest and most dedicated of buyers are still occasionally shopping the competition if for no reason other than to stay informed and keep you honest.

Practicing your sales skills may take on many forms. Here are just a few:

Live Practice

Depending on what it is you sell and how it is best sold, the best practice might be in real life. This follows the line of thinking that the best way to teach someone to swim is to throw them in the deep end and see what natural abilities come to the surface.

There really is no substitute for experience. The more real-world situations you find yourself in, the better and faster your skills will develop. You may find some of the most useful lessons are taught from not making sales, blowing leads and finding yourself in desperation. As necessity can be the mother of invention, the more you find yourself with chances to make a sale, the more likely you will develop the skills to do so.

Practicing Manno-a-Mirror!

So, you say blowing good leads isn't ideal, and you'd rather develop your skills without damaging prospects. As long as things have been sold, professional salespeople have looked in the mirror to reflect on how they are doing.

I do mean literally looking in the mirror to practice your sales presentation: remember, a huge portion of how you communicate is non-verbal. That being said, don't you think it's important to know how you look when you are "on-stage?"

Is there a better way to gesture as a way of articulating or emphasizing an important point? Does your body language exude confidence, competence and enthusiasm? When you see your presentation, is it energized, or will it lead to dozing and disinterest?

Is this Thing On?

Another way to practice, rehearse and review your sales tactics is to electronically record your "performance." The easiest time to do this is via telemarketing. Your prospect can't see that you're recording the call for future review. (Legal disclaimer: in some states there may be statutes against taping a phone call without the person on the other end knowing you are doing so.)

Videotaping a true sales encounter is far more complex. Therefore, most sales training that results from video training is done during role playing exercises. Most cell phones will have more than adequate cameras, so stick it in the corner and start your rehearsals!

Role Play

If you are not lucky enough to work for an organization that provides training and role-playing opportunities, you should seek out and create your own. This can be done in tandem with other reps on your staff or with people on your support team. If the workplace doesn't lend itself to roleplay, then recruit friends or relatives to help you. The important requirement is that they have an understanding that it's not a game, but an important part of your professional development.

The Best Offense is a Great Defense!

Among the many sales clichés you've probably heard is something along the lines of, "Objections are an invitation to keep digging for the sale." Through the discovery process, salespeople do plenty of digging and encounter many objections.

Smart salespeople practice their response to objections. In fact, the smartest ones anticipate objections and address them head-on, thus relieving the buyer's anxiety on the front side of a presentation.

You should periodically review a list of the common objections a given prospect may put before you. Objections may fall into any or all of these categories: durability, features, service, guaranty or warranty issues, timelines, company reputation, price, performance, training, complexity, site of production origin or shipping. Review the sales opportunities you've pursued and lost to come up with your own list. Also, review some that you have won and make note of how you overcame the objections to those sales.

This type of practice starts with being aware of the things you come up against. Then it implies that you prepare to meet those challenges in the future.

Skills Drills

To truly be successful in sales, as the cliché goes, you should "establish a repeatable set of actions that influence an identifiable outcome." In other words, figure out what works, and keep on doing that.

Your approach to sales should be broken up into chunks. These "steps to the sale" may include: prospecting, appointment setting, discovery, confirming the need, presenting your solution, asking for the order and maintaining the client relationship. For each step, can you identify the necessary skills?

For example, let's look just at "prospecting," the first of these skills. You can practice any or all of the following skill sets involved with prospecting: writing e-mails with differing value propositions or calls-to-action, telemarketing approaches, your personal commercial used at networking events, and even investing time in learning the best usage of social media for your product.

De-constructive Criticism!

For all of the practice techniques above, the best results will come from the staunchest of critics. Maybe that's you. Maybe it's your Sales Manager. Maybe it's your spouse. Or it could be a friend, a colleague, or a friendly client who provided candid feedback on your presentation.

The important thing is not to go through motions, but to understand the why, when, and how of employing certain sales techniques. Find someone who will rip apart and de-construct your presentation piece by piece, then tell you what worked, what didn't, and why. Without brutally candid feedback in your rehearsal phase, the real performance will most certainly suffer.

Olympic athletes dedicate years to training. For some, the difference between winning and losing will be measured in hundredths of a second or fractions of an inch. Practice will make the difference. None of the Olympic athletes want to say, "I almost got on the team," or, "I almost earned a medal."

As a sales rep, you don't want to be the one standing in a sales meeting or a review with your management saying, "we almost got that account," or, "they almost went with our proposal." Athletes want to win. To have the best chance at it, they practice diligently. If you want to be a sales winner, you too must frequently work out, push yourself to new limits and develop your skills to the best of your ability.

Skyline Exhibits occasionally brings together its worldwide organization for an event commonly referred to as "Expo." Smaller group meetings are held frequently, but "Expo" involves about 1,000 people, including manufacturing staff, corporate headquarters representatives and contingents from the field sales and distribution offices around the world.

Among the Expo highlights are several awards presentations and a commitment to recognition in the areas of design, service and sales. The big Saturday-night formal gala is reserved for announcing the Sales Excellence Awards. I was very proud when half of our sales staff won awards. Watching them take the stage to accept brought the cliché of "actors always rehearse" into more focus than ever.

Flanking a huge graphic backdrop and sharing a stage with two oversized projection screens were two 10' tall golden "Oscar" statues just like the ones on the Hollywood stage given out to actors, actresses and filmmakers. A strong voiceover announced the winners' career highlights, providing biographies illustrating their strengths.

Those golden statues serve as a reminder that this was a special moment to recognize achievement. The winners (commissioned salespeople) had already seen the glory in their paychecks, so this recognition was icing on the cake.

When Hollywood (or Broadway's Tony) next gives out awards, study how many awards are given out for parts you may describe as "intense." The intensity of an award-winning actor comes from mental preparation as well as rehearsal and putting one's energy, heart and soul into the process. The intensity of a winning sales rep can be no less a result of hours and years of practice.

Remember those doctors and lawyers that pull down the big bucks? Their professions refer to their businesses as a "law practice" or a "medical practice." Don't ever expect to win the gold if you don't invest in practicing your skills.

Up To Date

Strip Joint
New Orleans, LA

If you are a busy salesperson, you'll appreciate that this section of the book addresses three issues in a single chapter. Let's start with speaking "their language."

The first time I heard the expression, "I'm not buying a pig in a poke," I was clueless as to what my prospect was saying. It was in some General Manager's office at a TV Station in the South. There just weren't many (real) pigs in my Park Avenue New York office, nor on the subways, commuter train or roaming the Westchester suburbs where I lived. While I'm sure somewhere on Long Island where I grew up there must have been pigs, I had never poked any.

The phrase meant the GM was actually impressed with the presentation I had done and saw the value in acquiring the TV Programming package. However, he didn't want to buy something "sight unseen." Full comprehension of what your prospects say to you is a key ingredient to big sales.

Common language is more of an issue in the business world than ever before. The combination of several factors has led to the simple fact that those who are willing to invest in being multi-lingual will have a definite advantage over those who limit their communication skills to their native tongues.

For generations the children of immigrants from "the old country" grew up to speak English. Currently, there are massive numbers of Hispanic and Asian children born in America to parents for whom English remains a second language – or a mystery altogether. The immigration tide does not seem to be slowing, and some salesperson has to provide things for all these people.

The development of the euro-economy accelerated America's push for a series of international trade agreements such as NAFTA (the North American Free Trade Agreement). The movement of goods and services across international borders with fewer restrictions naturally leads to the need for international communication abilities. There are over 400 international trade agreements aimed at spurring business growth.

As referenced earlier, regrettably, some entire industries – such as textiles, once a dominant industry in the South – have migrated overseas, too. This has created a need for language skills to sell to or distribute in the US for overseas manufacturers.

Does it not make sense that your ability to converse in a prospect's native tongue will give you a leg up? Even the attempt to master a few words will be appreciated. The ability to effectively communicate on a business level will mean more gets sold. Also, the likelihood of costly errors resulting from miscommunication will be diminished.

I wish I were up to date on my language skills. Recently, in the span of a single week, I could have benefited greatly if I spoke Chinese, Italian, German and French. I guess learning to speak Southern wasn't good enough!

At a convention in New Orleans, I was out with some clients in the French Quarter. After dinner, we prowled through the wonderful debauchery that is N'awlins and wound up in a strip joint. From our table I could not only see the dancers on stage, but also who was entering the club.

The stripper on stage was beautiful (again, what you wear – or don't wear – needs to be appropriate to what you are selling). She was energetic, which is probably a requirement for swinging naked and spread-legged from a pole. Her body language was always under control. With the passing of time, while the specific image has faded from my mind, the thing that stands out was her language skills.

I saw a group of Japanese businessmen enter the club. They immediately took note of the stripper on stage. She, in turn, recognized an opportunity, and while still performing for the audience, spoke a few words in Japanese to the new arrivals.

In unison, their heads quickly began to nod, and their smiles broadened. In a moment, the stripper concluded her act and followed the Japanese clients to a private party room. Speaking their language helped make the sale!

The next aspect of remaining up to date that we'll discuss is technology. I remember sitting in the lobby of a West Palm Beach TV station in the mid 80's. The appointment before me was a rep from Paramount TV and his meeting with my client ran over. As they walked to the lobby, I was introduced to my competitor. I recall being in awe. He had a mobile cellular telephone!

For younger readers it may be hard to imagine that this was a big deal. But back then, not only was it a big deal, it was a big phone. The "bag phone" itself required a special case, and the permanently protruding antenna probably stuck out ten inches. At a "sleek" eight pounds, that was one cool gadget.

Some people are anti-technology. The owner of Medstar, in response to the sales staff's pleas for a database program (Act 1.0), proudly showed off his yellow pencil and legal pad. "Here is my computer screen," he said, holding up the pad. "Here is my keyboard," he gestured to the lead end of the pencil. "And here is my delete button," he showed us the eraser.

Some people are anti-technology because they've done fine without it. Some people are intimidated by it because they don't understand it. Some people just don't want to invest in it. As a business owner, I've learned that no matter how much or in what you invest, there is always a desire from someone on the team to have something more, something newer, something better.

As a salesperson, you have an obligation to your career to stay up to date with technology along two avenues. The first is what I'll term "generic tech stuff" (I'm not a very technical guy).

"Generic tech stuff" encompasses hardware and/or software non-specific to any particular industry. In addition to business-related applications, it may include things like knowing the difference between GB and RAM, or less drastically, the difference between a flat screen and a plasma TV. Generic tech stuff includes things like e-mail and the basic use of Word programs or spreadsheets.

Mastering "generic tech stuff" means you are comfortable with commonly-used technology. I'm no master – but I try to know enough and keep learning more so I'm never perceived as technologically illiterate by anyone other than my kids.

Babies are introduced to computers before they can walk. The smartphones in our pockets have more tech power than the first rockets launched to the moon. The need for a laptop, a cell phone, a scanner, a camera (video and stills, panorama, too, an electronic organizer, a watch (with stopwatch, timer, alarm clock, multi-time zone sensitivity) is satisfied by a single device. While they don't yet include microwaves, there are apps for delivery services of all kinds.

The other technology requirement for sales professionals in order to stay up to date is to steadfastly understand how technology impacts your business and your clients' business. You'd want to know if the fastest growing technology in your industry will make the product or service you are selling obsolete.

If you sell parts to the aviation industry, it stands to reason that sales skills alone won't cut it. You have to know how your product fits into the mechanics of making an airplane fly. The rep that sells copiers to the same airline buying pieces of planes has the same obligation to understand how his product fits into the airline's office technology scheme.

While it's obvious that a salesperson selling heart valves to medical facilities needs to be "up to date" on all technological and medical issues faced by her clients, the rep who sells the surgical gowns would also benefit from knowing how certain technology used in making the gowns produces a lighter, less constricting and more "breathable" gown. In other words, knowing the technology can provide a sales advantage. Not keeping up with the technology in your industry and your client's industry is a disadvantage.

The final element of keeping up to date puts the emphasis on the word *date.* My earlier words on technology and language dealt with staying current. This is a few lines on "dating!"

When I first started representing Skyline Displays, I attended a training session that brought together salespeople from around the country. One night, a colleague from my company and I had dinner with two reps from a Florida distributorship.

A woman we barely knew openly and graphically shared her methods of closing a few big deals. Throughout my career, I'll admit to having asked both clients and vendors for favors – but not the kinds of favors involving the proverbial knee-pads.

I have asked clients, staff and vendors to bare their souls, expose their needs and reveal their secrets. But never to bare their breasts, drop their pants or take one for the team!

Were this an isolated occurrence, it wouldn't warrant inclusion in this book. But the fact is that there are reps who use sex – and sexuality – to sell.

Movies and TV shows are filled with clichéd stories of corporations providing hookers for favored clients. While I have no personal experience in this endeavor, I have come to accept that clichés are clichés because there is a strong element of truth to them.

One of the problems with trading sex for a deal is that the product you are selling usually has to last longer than the sex. Ultimately, your client will determine what sort of negotiating you must do to "earn" their repeat business!

Furthermore, going back to the importance of referrals, it's important to ask ourselves what is it that we want our clients to say about us.

Beyond the lurid sex for the sale topic, innocent dating and legitimate relationships can lead to awkward business associations. If you start dating a client and he or she decides to buy products or services elsewhere, what strain does that put on the personal relationship? If the personal relationship dissolves, what does that do to the professional relationship?

This is a book about sales, and while that topic has everything to do with morality, this is not the place for a detailed discussion on dating. It is, however, the absolute place to remind my readers there is a difference between a "quid pro" and a "sales pro!"

Go Out On A High Note

Storage facilities
Istanbul & Brazil

W hen I was selling television programming, it was just as important to maintain good relationships with the stations that didn't buy from me as with those that did. The world of TV syndication meant that you had a very narrow client base to sell to. At that point in time, in all but the largest of markets it was rare to have more than four potential stations to buy from you.

Given the type of program, series or programming package you were selling, your prospects might be narrowed to two or three per market. Ironically, often the TV Stations who could most afford or offered the best time periods for a show were the ones with the least amount of need.

If a station didn't buy or cancelled something they had carried for a period of time, you couldn't afford to make an enemy because you'd undoubtedly need them again.

The same concept of not burning bridges holds true now, as I work in an industry with seemingly limitless prospects. Almost every industry has trade shows. I can sell to the public sector or the private sector. I can sell to non-profits or for-profit companies. I can sell to firms that offer service and firms that make tangible products.

Despite the wealth of prospects, it remains important not to burn bridges. Shortly after I joined The Oliver Group, I was approached by a startup company with big dreams but low budgets. They asked me to develop a large, multi-unit proposal running to hundreds of thousands of dollars, and as they were in the process of going public, assured me they'd have the money.

I spent a lot of time on the project, only to never see it fully presented. I was angry and resented the company. But periodically I'd stay in touch, and occasionally made some small sales to them. Even with every positive encounter, I never forgot the loss. Today they are one of my most active accounts. Had I expressed my anger twenty-five years ago, I'd have shot myself in the foot and would now be hobbling instead of dancing on cloud nine.

Another company that we worked with makes robots for production automation. Our initial attempts to land their business failed. The failures were frustrating, as we felt we had great solutions to truly help them.

About two years after they decided to buy a less expensive offering, they called to discuss moving forward with a new project. Even though they had not bought our initial proposal, we made a positive impression and much of what we forewarned them about came true. Initially, when we were told about the loss, the rep involved went ballistic and it was all I could do to keep her from verbally (or physically) assaulting the prospect. By going out on a high note, we instead laid the foundation for future business.

One of the more frustrating losses I've encountered occurred as a result of a corporate merger. First Union and Wachovia banks announced merger plans shortly after we were awarded a preferred supplier contract with First Union. We were handling exhibits and displays at trade shows and special events all around the world. We were storing and managing a large arsenal of displays we had created and an even larger group of displays they owned that were created by our competitors.

When the merger plans were announced, we held the account for months, but once it was finalized, virtually everything, from who supplied the banks with paper clips to what company would provide their employees with health insurance was put out to competitive bid. The hours and days we spent on our response to their request for a proposal were numerous, intense and ultimately in vain.

Not only were we on the losing side of the bid for a piece of business, but we had come to enjoy the level of billings the account was bringing in. After some minor wound licking, I determined we needed to go out on a high note if we ever wanted the chance to win back parts of the newly merged bank's business. When we had first won the account and taken it from an exhibit house in Philadelphia, they had been jerks about cooperating in the transfer of assets. I don't believe they were given the chance to bid on the merged company's RFP.

We did everything possible to assist with cataloging materials and shipping of assets. We provided parts and answered questions. Whether or not the "whole enchilada" contract came up for bid again any time in the future was not the issue. I knew there would be a significant amount of need that wouldn't fall under that contract, and we were in their backyard to meet those needs. So, if you're an executive at Wachovia and you have an exhibit need, remember, we went out on a high note!

It's not just the potential for business with a company that has rejected you that calls for going out on high note. There are other reasons to do so.

The combination of ever-decreasing employment tenure, mergers and acquisitions, spin-offs and start-ups means the person who rejects you today at one company could tomorrow be either your boss or your biggest customer. Either way, you don't want them thinking you're the cry-baby who never got the memo that in sales, you win some, you lose some.

Remember too, the critical importance of the "Law of Two Hundred," which says everyone knows two hundred people. So what do you want the one prospect you've just angrily called a "son of a bitch" because he didn't buy from you to tell his two hundred buddies? He could say you're unstable, overly emotional, dangerous and to be avoided at all costs. Or, he could say, "You know, even though I wound up going with another company on this piece of business, I'd surely give them a chance next time around."

One of the first large displays I did was for a machinery company in a 3,000 square foot exhibit space. At that time, our product was adaptable to large environments but not necessarily ideal for them. The project sold, the booth went up, the show went off without any major problems.

The US office of this particular company exhibited only every four years at a Quadrennial Trade Show. The next time the event rolled around, they rented an exhibit from the show's contractor and we were never in the running. I was angry and frustrated. Making matters worse, the company's facility is located right on the interstate, so I pass them often and always wondered what we could have done better, differently, etc.

When I saw them at the show using an exhibit system from a competitor, I wanted to charge up to the owner, demand an explanation and for good measure tell him his company looked like crap.

But, I held my tongue. Instead, we periodically kept in touch with the company and tried to include them on mailings about new product introductions and vast, quickly accumulating experience in large exhibit environments. As luck would have it, with a shift in the show date of the Quadrennial Exhibition they attend, a trade show booth their parent company in Europe owned was possibly not going to be available to the US subsidiary.

Half of it was in Brazil, half in Istanbul. Immediately following the show that the US group was to attend, both those halves needed to be in China. All of a sudden, the company was faced with huge shipping and air freight fees if they wanted to use their owned asset. As an alternative, they asked us to propose a rental solution.

Had I voiced my irritation, we wouldn't have been considered to fulfill a large need. Go out on a high note. Hold your tongue. And even if you lose a sale, don't lose the chance to make a big sale in the future!

Shit Happens

3:45AM
French Quarter, New Orleans

Emblazoned on a t-shirt displayed in the window of a novelty shop in New Orleans, I discovered one of life's great truisms. It was late at night, or early in the morning. Years back, there were times the distinction between the two got blurred.

Exhibiting a convention, the daily schedule often included early-morning client breakfasts, seminars and general sessions which were then followed by six or eight hours of working a trade show.

This was followed by meeting for drinks, client or company dinners, industry receptions or private party blow-outs. Finally, on the final night in town, our staff was parading through Bourbon Street. We were spent, in every manner possible – physically exhausted, mentally drained, corporately on cloud nine with the feeling that we'd given all there was to give.

Most of the people I closely worked with at Group W I came to love, admire, respect and enjoy being with. We were making money, saving the world (our projects had a community service aspect), and often cerebrally challenging one another. This particular night, after imbibing in some green concoction at a place called "The Dungeon," we were tackling a light brainteaser: "What is the meaning of life?"

163

And there it was! Hanging in a window, the answer was staring us in the face on the front of a T-shirt: Shit Happens. And just as in life, in sales, shit happens.

There are elements to every rep's professional life that they can control. Unfortunately, we can't control every aspect of our lives. If we could, I'm thinking our closing percentages would all be much, much, higher!

One time, I was pursuing a client in the South Carolina Lowcountry. The company was on the fringes of the medical field involved with diagnostic testing. From Greenville to their office was about three and a half hours. I visited with the VP of Marketing on several trips to the area.

After a few visits, it was closing time. Despite a late in the day meeting, I was determined not to leave without a signed contract. After a number of adjustments to both my proposed solution and their available budget, we agreed on a deal, signed the papers and both of us were anxious to get home. Of course, he had a 15-minute ride and mine was several hours. Therefore, we agreed we'd speak the following day to work through some of the production decisions which were separate and apart from the contractual business decisions we had just concluded.

When I phoned the next afternoon and asked for my client, the receptionist curtly asked, "Who is calling and what is it in reference to?" It was not their usual manner of answering the phone. Sales paranoia set in. Perhaps the client was having second thoughts and screening calls to avoid me? No, it was worse. He was dead. A car accident on his way home from work the night before… shit happens.

Raleigh, Durham and Chapel Hill, North Carolina form an area referred to RTP – or, the Research Triangle Park area. The concentration of universities coupled with an entrepreneurial spirit and great public sector/private sector partnerships helped the region enjoy accelerated growth during the rise of the dot.com bubble.

The commercialization of the internet made many people rich. But it made many more people rich on paper, and for many, that paper is now worthless. Too many companies started with an idea, obtained financing, rifled through monies available, and went belly-up without ever making either a product or a sale.

Our Raleigh, NC office enjoyed the dot.com bubble while it lasted. Companies were in need of quickly capturing market share so they'd want to make a big splash at a trade show with a fancy exhibit. At times, our reps there were so busy with new dot.com clients, they didn't have time – or didn't make time – for others. The pipeline was dry. Then, the dot.com bubble burst. Shit happens.

With the exception of the Chairman of the Federal Reserve, we can't control the economy. And even he can't do it alone. When terrorists strike in New York, oil prices rise in the Middle East. Rising fuel prices make the cost of doing business greater. Fewer capital purchases are made. News of a crumbling economy becomes rampant. Individual consumers are slower to make purchases. On the whole, "that darned world" plays a big role in whether or not you'll make quota. Shit happens.

As a sales rep, you may do everything perfectly. Let's say that after investing many hours in a project, you make the sale. Unfortunately, a strike at a subsidiary of your prospect in a remote place halfway around the world initiates a company-wide spending freeze. Or, the contact you've worked with for months gets a new job and leaves. Shit happens.

You and your next repeat sale are only as good as the team that stands behind you. The ability of your organization to fulfill the services sold or provide the products contracted for is directly linked to your paycheck. I remember a project when there was a custom graphic element to a client's project that we felt would be both more affordable and better fulfilled by a provider other than our normal vendor.

The supplier we worked with showed us incredible examples of finished samples. We toured their facilities and our design engineers spoke at length with their production people on integrating their product into the display we were fabricating for a highly visible, very important client.

Some small issues got us nervous early in the process. But every time we raised a question, they had an answer and alleviated our concerns. Their sales rep did a good job, except he ultimately over-promised and under-delivered. The finished product they provided was sub-par. At great expense and with little time, we made corrections so what we fulfilled to our client was acceptable.

That graphics company couldn't stand behind the claims its rep made. The salesperson had worked hard to earn our business. The company lost because they had a rep over-selling. The rep lost because he had a company under-delivering.

I only had two disappointing moments during my years with Group W. One was when a project I had developed, called "Thanks to Teachers," culminated in a Washington reception with White House involvement. In remarks to the crowd at the banquet, the Chairman of Group W TV thanked "my boss and her staff" but didn't mention me by name. Although childish, I was disappointed.

The other was when a bean-counter was subsequently made our division head and offered a $2,500 incentive bonus for hitting certain quotas. I surpassed mine and he decided not to pay. I left Group W shortly thereafter. His miserly decision left a bad taste in my mouth as well as the rest of the staff (don't ever believe there are secrets).

The bean counter was guilty of the same thing as the rep for the graphics company. They committed the sin of over promising and under delivering. But shit happens.

As a sales rep, you can't control all that goes on around you. However, to your clients, you are the public face of your company, its suppliers and its staff. A great rule to keep "shit" like this from happening is the following: under promise and over deliver. It's a much better formula for achieving big sales.

Absolute Trust

W hen you say you'll do something, do you do it?

It's simple enough to see that if a client or a prospect makes a request, you will want to follow up, promptly, as promised. But, do you? There are so many details on some projects, dropping just one of the many balls you're juggling may not matter. But if that one little ball is an important one to your client, you'll know soon enough.

What you may not learn to recognize right away is the resulting collateral damage to how they perceive you. Maybe you didn't get back to them when you said you would. Maybe you committed to send an example of something and got busy then forgot. These little omissions may not be earth shattering, but they are threats to your relationship.

Relationships are built on trust. Client relationships implicitly dictate that the buyer has faith you will do what you say, when you say it will be done. Sales reps the world-over should zealously guard and protect that bond of trust and not do anything to break it.

Let's say someone on your support team in the midst of a busy day reminds you, "Hey, I need that information…" If you tell them you'll get to it right away, but your day spirals out of control and that little request gets buried, did you lie? Did you really mean to sabotage your own good name in their minds?

Everyone gets busy. Everyone has shifting priorities. If you damage the trust between yourself and your team, how can you expect them to have faith that you'll hold up your end of the bargain (i.e. to bring in the money that pays their salaries)? The smallest amount of doubt in their mind can mean you are no longer getting your proper share of their efforts.

Say the boss asks for a report, perhaps because their boss needs it, and you promise to get to it by day's end, but a prospect also makes a request – who comes first? If you choose the prospect and don't fulfill the commitment to the boss, regardless of the reason or excuse, what does it do to your reliability in the boss's mind?

If you submit sales forecasts and projections that consistently fall short or bear little resemblance to your actual activity, what does that do to the boss's perception of your reliability, or worse, your knowledge of your own client activity? Does it plant the idea that there may be other areas where the rep is incompetent? Even in the slightest way, can it suggest that what the rep says cannot be trusted? And, does that pose a question in your boss's head as to whether clients trust you?

A company must have absolute trust in the people that represent it to the marketplace. The company must be assured that the rep is not only doing the correct things, but also giving their best effort. Ideally, management techniques can determine the extent of the effort being put forth. Ultimately, results will tell the story. However, speaking on behalf of sales managers and owners everywhere, life is too short to ever have to worry about whether you can trust a rep.

Of course, trust can be shattered in the other direction as well. A huge number of sales reps I interview are in the market for a job because they feel their current employer has let them down.

Companies can betray the trust a rep has in them in many ways. The performance of a service the rep had sold to a client could be inadequate, thus damaging the rep's reputation. The quality of a product can be other than what a company has asked a sales person to communicate to prospects. Again, not only is the company's image tarnished, but the salesman's professional credentials receive a black mark, too.

If an employer makes a promise to a salesperson regarding "training to be provided" or "incentive rewards to be paid out," then fails to do so, they damage trust. Despite blaming cash flow, the market, timing or some other excuse, the fact remains that a promise has not been lived up to. Even if most things the company says it will do are done, the difference is that absolute trust has been damaged forever and can never be repaired.

When I'm with other sales managers, we'll swap stories of how reps have lied themselves out of a job. Here are two personal favorites. Sometimes I wonder how dumb people think their bosses are.

A rep worked for me in a satellite office. In the course of a normal month I'd only be there between two and five days. My first clue that there was a problem arose when she needed off for Grandma's funeral. Then Gramps, poor Gramps, passed several weeks later.

Then – would you believe the unbearable luck this family was having – Aunt Gertie was ill, on her deathbed, and had nobody else to care for her. My rep just needed to go and be with her aunt for a few days.

When a rep is on full commission, it's hard to say no when someone is hitting their numbers and needs time off. In this case, the rep was ahead of her quota as a result of two rather large sales. Those sales were from companies outside our normal territory, but the buyers were "personal associates" of the rep, so she pursued them and closed some good business for us.

Other reps that worked in her office were fed up with the daily abuses of responsibility she evidenced with them but cleaned up when I would come to town. But one day, she forgot to clean some Vodka bottles from her car seat. Then she submitted a call report and I followed a hunch!

With one call to a prospect she had supposedly met with the prior week, I learned the meeting was fabricated on her call report. Several others, too, were meetings in her own mind and on a report for my benefit! At the same time, another grandparent was taken ill. While she was supposedly visiting "PaPa," she was actually on a cross-country motorcycle trip with a boyfriend. It turned out he was also the buyer in one of the large deals she had closed.

She'd have had to have lots of boyfriends to hit her quota consistently! But, even if she was a top rep, she'd still have been let go. Her crime wasn't not selling, nor was it selling to a boyfriend. It wasn't any one particular made-up meeting when she wasn't where she said she'd been. She simply couldn't be trusted. Her tears and promises to "never lie again" were just pitiful.

This next breach of trust is so surreal you won't believe it. But it's true! A rep, who never should have been hired in the first place, for weeks indicated he was pursuing a meeting with a golf tourism company in Myrtle Beach to sell them an exhibit. The company was called Gary Player Golf.

At that time, Gary Player, the world-renowned professional golfer, was still active on the Champions circuit of the PGA. He was the oldest player to ever make "the cut" at the Masters, doing so at age 62. Like many professional athletes, he had business interests and/or endorsement deals beyond the immediate scope of playing their sport.

The rep was having a hard time nailing down the meeting. Finally, on a Friday evening, he came to my office and exclaimed that they agreed to meet with him, but it would have to be on Saturday morning, the next day. I wished him well on his meeting and eagerly awaited a report on the following Monday.

While I wasn't part of my rep's discussions with Gary Player Golf, I'm 100% certain he wasn't speaking with Gary – especially that weekend. When I saw the rep on Monday, he told me the meeting went great and they had interest in some displays. He said it went so well that they all went out to breakfast after the meeting. He said that Gary was there to put in his feelings on the project. Then, Gary stayed and had breakfast with them, too.

It was all I could do not to erupt. But I figured if this guy was dumb enough to lie about something so blatantly untrue, I needed to test the limits of his stupidity. So, I got a copy of Monday's paper – the day they report the sports results from the weekend.

This was the weekend Gary Player won The Senior British Open.

I called the rep back to my office and feigned excitement. I screamed down the hall, "Come here, quickly, you're in the paper." He ran in to my office and asked, "What's it say?" So I made-believe I was reading aloud an article, "Gary Player has done it again! He's added to his over 160 career championships by winning the Senior British Open this weekend at Royal Portrush in Northern Ireland."

I paused to see the look on the rep's face, then continued, "Player, in a statement, decreed the match was tougher than normal. In addition to the competition on the course, he had to fly back and forth across the ocean for a breakfast meeting in Myrtle Beach."

Obviously, Player didn't fly. Neither did the rep's story. He was gone that day.

Way back in the 1700s, author and playwright Henry Fielding said, "It is a good maxim to trust a person entirely or not at all."

Will It Go On The Fridge?

Kitchens
Across the Country
Forever!

There is a business management concept, practice, and application called "Six Sigma." The essence of the concept is to measure activity to enable an organization to better manage its resources and achieve defined goals.

If corporations can apply analytical management tools to everything from the effect of currency fluctuations to paper clip usage by the shipping department, then sales people (because we're smart) can devise a measurement strategy for our activities, too. I've recently put a new emphasis on this within my company and what I'm learning is fascinating, beneficial and scary.

The saying goes, "You can't manage what you don't measure." Let's begin with the admonition that regardless of whether you have a boss, an owner or a sales manager to whom you report, the responsibility for "managing you" is *yours*.

Don't look to others to establish measurable goals or a defined matrix of activities to manage. Do it yourself. All it can do is add money to your commissions, and that's fun to count!

The second admonition is that you have to be careful not to create a management tool that becomes a chore unto itself. The idea here is not to take away from productive time by putting some bureaucratic tracking tool in place.

What we want to do is define the activities that are pertinent to your success as a sales rep and then have you "manage" yourself towards those activities. Ideally, information and/or processes that are already an intrinsic part of your daily activity will lend themselves to being monitored and measured.

Before confusing you further, let me illustrate a simple example of what I'm talking about: suppose you knew or determined that to hit the revenue goals necessary for your personal or corporate responsibilities, it mandated twenty face-to-face meetings with new prospects during a month. Now, let's say that for several months running, your sales numbers were down. The danger most reps fall into is not realizing they are on a negative spiral until it has already occurred.

By using some form of what I call "metrics measurement," you can avoid the death spiral. Instead of seeing a three month trend of less-than-quota sales after they've occurred, you could instead determine halfway through the first month that the number of appointments you have set for the coming weeks will be inadequate to hit your goals. Now there is still time for corrective, pro-active action.

Unlike many other professionals, sales reps are used to getting a regular "report card" in the form of "how we did" for a given month, quarter, day, week or year. Usually we'll get an understanding of how our performance has stacked up against either the competition, the other reps on our team, and/or the company's expectations for our productivity.

However, only the luckiest of sales reps receive useful activity measurement indicators in a timely fashion that will help them manage their actions in a successful direction. If you work for a company that has dedicated the necessary software, training and sales management resources to helping you manage your activity, count yourself lucky and *don't* resent it. Use it to your advantage and thank the sales gods you've been blessed with these tools.

If you work for a company that is solely focused on your output, then more than ever, it's up to you to devise a metrics management system that works for your circumstances. When constructing your activity measurement indicators, here are two things you must consider:

1) You can't ignore the fact that results matter.
2) You can't ignore the fact that sustaining positive results is the outcome of repeating defined successful activities.

Which of the following factors could help you in managing your sales?

Knowing how much you've sold in a specific time frame? By measuring your sales within a specific timeframe, whether weekly, monthly, daily or annually, can you pinpoint trends and/or recurring opportunities?

Does it make a difference discerning between those orders you've written versus orders for which you've collected payments and/or begun production or performing service? For many reps, these kinds of breakdowns yield important information that effect when they will collect their commissions.

Is it helpful to know how many calls you have made or on-line campaigns you've launched? Since sales is a numbers game and often the process begins by "smiling and dialing," knowing you are making calls can be positive reassurance that you are priming the pump. Recognizing early in the process that you've been so busy on fulfillment issues that you're not making calls helps you avoid a cavity in your commissions later on.

Also, if you can recognize you're making the calls, but perhaps not getting the required number of appointments indicated on your "metrics tracker," perhaps that is a signal that what you are saying or doing during the telemarketing activity needs modification.

Similarly, if you define that "x" number of discovery meetings per month are needed or desirable, and you are attaining or overachieving x but aren't making the sales the way you used to, it could be a sign that either the product is tired or your sales interaction techniques need an overhaul. The key is that without measuring and knowing you are making the calls or setting the appointments, it's harder to pinpoint what is in need of a fix.

Would it be helpful to know the ratio or mix of new clients vs. repeat business? First of all, you should always know the origin of your sales. What if unbeknown to you, 95% of the people that purchased from you did so because you wore green socks? Wouldn't you wear them every day? What if you spent 90% of your time making door-to-door cold calls but three quarters of the people who purchased from you did as a result of multi-touch e-mail campaigns? Wouldn't you want to waste less shoe leather and spend more time on computer prospecting?

By measuring where our business comes from and reviewing it quarterly, we can see that anywhere from 58% to 79% of our business are repeat clients. In general, my industry sees about two thirds repeat business. If the trend is on the high-side, I know it's time to crack the whip to focus on new business development. If we come in low, as long as our overall numbers are growing I view it as positive, because we're just expanding the base for future repeaters. If we've come in low *and* had a bad quarter, however, we need to revisit some old friends!

When we initiated a formal "activity management indicator," or metrics management plan, one of the indicators we looked at was contact with existing clients. Among the most revealing stats was that we were effectively ignoring two thirds of our business!

Database, marketing automation and customer relationship management software tools can help your measurements become almost automatic. If you're radically anti-tech, just keep a clean calendar and contact lists. Whether high tech or low tech, the important thing is to start by defining the activities that lead to sales, set goals for those activities, then measure progress towards those goals on a regular basis.

When I developed the metrics tracker program for my company, we added a contest component to make it more palatable for the reps. The contest was based on points measured on the tracker. Each month, every "activity indicator" was reviewed against a pre-determined goal. Reps could over-index on a particular indicator and get extra points. Or, if they only achieved (for instance) half their goal for that indicator, they'd only receive half the available points for that category. In this manner, the "rep report card" can help correct behavior, not just give a singular total of what was sold.

Throughout the world, when children come home from school with a gold star on their tests or straight A's on their report cards, the positive news goes up on the fridge! I challenge you to create your own sales report card. When you overachieve, put that "report card" on the fridge and tell the kids to take you out for ice cream!

PART 3

Sales Fallacies

Time Management Really Is BS

Electronic Components Company
Anywhere, USA

Take this quick exam:

How many of you have a computer?

How many of you utilize a database or some type of CRM (Customer Relationship Management) software?

How many of you have voicemail?

How many of you have a microwave?

How many of you have a cell phone?

How many of you have an e-mail account?

Okay, now the big bonus question: how many of you using these "time-saving" devices actually have more time?

Let me tell you about Diane and Harold, two reps that work for the same distributor of specialized electronic components. They both started with their company at the same time, which was about six years ago. The company operates with an open territory and protected accounts policy, meaning any rep can sell into any geography, to any company, as long as another rep is not already working with the account. (Larger nationwide accounts and subsidiary companies are treated as unique, individual companies.)

Diane and Harold went through the same training programs and have an identical approach to marketing and administrative support. After a phased down 12-month period of being on salary, then salary with a draw against commissions, their salary became all commission-based (with a draw). Their average compensation over the last three fiscal years was not identical. Diane grossed, on average, $134,641. Harold grossed $63,117.

Let's look at their typical workdays. According to company policy, the hours are from 8:30 AM to 5:00 PM for salaried staff. Although sales reps don't punch a clock, they are expected to put in the full day (although some leeway is allowed, given their odd travel hours and occasional need to be working on presentations at home).

Harold is into family and fitness. Whenever possible, he will take his kids to school. It's a ritual that enriches his life. Barring any traffic snags, he can make it to the office by 8:35 or 8:40 AM. Once he powers up his computer, he downloads some e-mails and dedicates fifteen to twenty minutes perusing industry-related websites.

At 9:00 AM, Harold assembles a daily to-do list and a quarter of an hour later is generally doing an office walkabout meeting with administrators, the shipping department, and manufacturing to ensure all of his clients' orders have shipped correctly or are moving through the production process. He'll generally have some follow up work from the previous afternoon's appointments, too.

With some answers to potential questions in hand, Harold can now get on the phone with some existing clients to address any issues related to their orders. As long as he's now in a phone mode, usually at about 11:00 AM he'll make some new prospect calls or follow up on e-mail campaigns. By 11:50 at least four days a week, he makes sure he's in the car headed to the gym.

His workouts are kept to under an hour, allowing for a quick shower and grabbing some healthy take-out to bring back and eat at the desk. When possible, he schedules local and regional appointments for the afternoons. This way, once he's out and about, he doesn't need to return to the office. Occasionally, at 5pm he'll meet his wife at her office across from the park for a few minutes of some quiet time before they pick up the kids at daycare and attend to soccer, baseball games, and dance classes.

Diane also has two kids in school and daycare. As a single mom, she really appreciates the flexibility that comes with a sales career and the opportunity it provides her to earn an above-average income. She does, however, admit to occasional moments of guilt about not having more time for the kids – or, for that matter, herself!

Her day also includes exercise, and she credits it with keeping her sane! At 5:30 AM, she's aerobicizing or riding a stationary bike while watching CNN before getting the kids up at 6:30. She takes advantage of dropping the kids at their school as early as allowed and is usually at her desk at 7:30. By 7:45, she's reviewed the to-do list prepared the previous night, scanned e-mails and listened to any voicemail messages. Texts usually get responded to immediately upon arrival.

Usually there is about an hour of paperwork, but by 9:00 AM she is on the phone setting new client appointments. She'll allow about ninety minutes in her morning schedule for this because she also assigns herself the task of filling appointment slots at 10:30 and 11:45 each day. If any of the internal staff needs her for problems with her clients, she tries to meet with them while many clients are lunching.

By 1:30, she likes to be back on the phones or computer for another 90-minute session, except for on Fridays, when she's found a high number of prospects take the afternoon off. For that reason, she challenges herself to get pre-set appointments all Friday afternoon to ensure those hours are maximized.

She will try to set up one or two afternoon appointments and has made a game of doing her notes and related paperwork with her kids while they do their "homework." However, weekends are generally sacred family time.

Diane and Harold live in the same community and exist in the same twenty-four hour universe. Yet, her income more than doubles his. What are the key differences? It is not how they manage "time." They have the same time. It is how they manage their activities and utilize support systems available. It is how they prioritize and even sacrifice.

Whereas Harold chooses to make family and exercise his priority, Diane finds a way to make family commitments fit with her need for more income. Both are good people. It's simply that one is making more money.

None of Harold's' actual work time is wasted. There are just things he insists on doing that could be handled by others, freeing up time to sell more. Diane makes a priority of scheduling more client appointments and scheduling the time to make the calls to set those appointments.

Too many sales professionals find solace in bragging about being busy and being challenged by the elusive goal of better time management. It is absurd to think you can manage time. We all have the same 24 hours in a day. Sorry, no exceptions.

It's what you do with your time that matters.

A Good Salesperson
Can Sell Anything

Larchmont Acres
Larchmont, NY

When Ellen was pregnant with our first child, we put our co-op apartment up for sale. After nine months of pregnancy and a year and a half with a crib in our living room, we took the apartment off the market and became landlords. Thirty-two years later, we still own it.

It started with his grandmothers. They were convinced the boy was gorgeous. His unbiased grandfathers, aunts, uncles and even parents all agreed. With the concurrence of some friends, neighbors and the occasional passerby in a crowd, we were easy targets when we received a query from a local child modeling agency.

In our minds, word of our son's unique, debonair looks had certainly reached the halls of the modeling agency. Of course, in reality, they had bought our name on some list from a parenting magazine to which we subscribed.

I couldn't have been more excited and anxious over our seven-month-old's "interview" with the modeling scout. Francois wore all black. He was thin, artsy and spoke at a quick pace about the many opportunities available to child models. He took us on a mental tour of our child's certain fame and fortune. It would start with magazine and newspaper ads. Then, there would be the TV commercials with lifetime residual checks. The TV series and feature films would inevitably follow.

Primed, excited and proud we eagerly poured over the representation agreement. Small print was hardly a concern when you had a diaper-clad future star in the corner of your living room. Then, we discussed the head shots and test photo shoot. For only $795 we'd be on our way to parenting fame and fortune.

Something wasn't right. If our little bundle of blockbuster magic was such a sure thing, why would the agency feel it necessary to charge us to take his pictures? By the time we booted Francois from the apartment we were relatively sure his name was Frank and the closest he got to models was carrying the fashion section of the Times under his arm.

Was it a scam? Not in the legal sense. But was it a method of selling child photo services that played on hopes and ambition with little truth to support the claims? Likely. Could *I* sell it? Could I go into people's homes and tap into their most precious possession's potential? Hell, no.

When I first joined The Oliver Group, we had a rep who was regularly, verbally abused and berated by a former manager. In fact, that manager wouldn't even allow this rep to go by the nickname he'd been using all his life. This poor guy was so beaten down under poor management that there was no way he'd ever thrive in front of a customer.

Six or eight months into his tenure with our company, "Chip" left. Several years later, when I was in management, Chip phoned soliciting business for his present company. After leaving our display firm, he went back into selling computer software. He thrived. He understood the product, its capabilities and how to present its benefits to prospects.

About that same time, we had another rep who was a young guy that struggled with selling our product. Without a daily call quota, he found any excuse not to make calls or set appointments. When he did have prospects, he didn't instill confidence in them. He was not successful selling our product.

But he had built up some friendships in the company and several on the staff saw him socially. He went to work for an Auto Magazine and rose to a sales management position. Was his success a result of him being different? While we're all evolving on a regular basis, the difference was more one of circumstances. He was dealing with a different product, a different target audience and a different sales methodology.

I think back to my last months with Medstar and the entirety of my time with WHNS-TV. I had been successful in sales prior to that point and since that time. Same guy, different results.

Being promoted to a sales management position rudely interrupted my grand plan for living in a small town and being home every night by 5:30. Ultimately, this led to increased management responsibilities and overseeing daily operations of our five offices in three states while maintaining my own sales accounts.

Travel was a constant part of the job. I'm not complaining, but a full-time sales job coupled with full-time management responsibilities means either the company is poorly run, my sales will never reach their potential, or life outside of work will certainly be sacrificed. While any and all of those things may be true on a day to day basis, one certainty is that by the end of a road trip, I'd usually be exhausted.

One Thursday evening, I returned home after a trip to Virginia. It was already approaching 9:00 PM. Thoughts of my butt on my couch, hugs from the kids, and relaxation were my motivation for the last hours of the drive home. Ellen met me with those loving words, "Oh good, you made it in time. The Vacuum guy is coming at nine."

Ding Dong. 9:00 PM, and smiley Brad the hyper vacuum salesperson is at our door. The kids are shooed away. It's serious sales pitch time. Brad has one or two carefully-prepared statements, then reaches into his bag of tricks and removes a jar of mud. He dumps it on our rug. I didn't care how well his vacuum sucked, unless it had the ability to give me a massage and pour me a drink, quickly, there was nothing being sold that night.

Could I go into people's homes and annoy them after long hard days? No, not me. More power to you, Brad.

When Kara, our daughter, was ten years old, she had already played soccer for five years. Between spring and fall teams, she had played in several leagues. The dominant league in town was St. Giles Soccer and they had a facility called Mesa Fields. Over the years, we'd seen Mesa grow and grow. Parent volunteers from all teams help staff the snack stand and the merchandise shop.

The volunteer assignments generally only lasted about two hours in duration. Food duty isn't too bad, as there is a steady flow of cold spectators in need of hot chocolates and hungry two-game-a-day players needing a hot dog. The merchandise shop is another story.

It wouldn't be unheard of to spend two hours in the merchandise shack without a customer. Somehow, by the second or third week of a season, the shirts, shorts and car magnets that are the required uniform of a proper "soccer mom" have all been purchased. When I was "volunteered" for shack duty, my mind raced to devise methods of growing its business:

1) Could we sell more by having vendors walking some prime stuff to the sidelines of all twenty fields?
2) What if we gave coupons with incentives to the thousands of attendees each weekend to drive them into the store?
3) What about a different guest star signing autographs in the store each weekend?

The act of waiting for customers to come to you that is inherent to retail sales probably rules me out for that career, too!

It is a fallacy that great sales people can sell anything. Great salespeople have an understanding of what they are good at and what they can adapt to. They search for a repeatable methodology to profitably sell a product about which they are passionate.

Born Salesman Really Is BS

Duke Medical Center
Durham, NC

Hey, have you heard this one? Two babies are lying in their bassinets in the newborn ward at the hospital. The first one turns to its newborn neighbor and says, "So, what's your quota?" That's not the way salespeople develop!

I am always in awe of parallels between sports and business. When I see on a resume that someone has been involved in competitive sports, they warrant an extra look. Like much of the sports world, sales is about competition, winning and losing. It takes grit, determination, drive, skill, brains and practice.

The concept of a "natural-born athlete" often strikes me as an affront to the thousands of hours athletes spend working out, exercising and practicing their sport. Perhaps the genetics were good and the aptitude was in place, but surely Olympians, professional athletes and even the ten year old soccer player spending hours in the backyard all practice to develop their abilities.

Many a salesperson is born out of necessity. An entrepreneurial drive leads to an idea, giving birth to a company. Then, it has to be sold. Some salespeople find themselves thrust into the position when their former marketing positions are outsourced. They know the product, the company and the clients. Now, their choice is to be on the streets selling or stranded on the unemployment line. Sales it is!

Many salespeople who do exceptionally well start out in a technical mode. Their attention to detail, their intense product knowledge and their experience communicating the product benefits to others lends itself to a sales function. Ask a sales professional who has a technical or engineering background if a sales career was in their plans and the likelihood is the answer will be "no." Not only was it not ordained from the cradle, it wasn't on their radar after college or grad school or even into their first few jobs.

Some view the "born salesman" as the gregarious, back slapping guy who is everyone's buddy. Some view him as the slick, polished, well-connected professional that was always in the right place at the right time. And some are surprised when the wall flower blossoms into a sales dynamo. How does that happen?

Could it be because good salespeople are observant? Could it be because by letting others talk and not shoving their opinions down people's throats, they learn more and get honest answers from those around them?

Sales professionalism involves training. Training can be formal or informal, but it must be constant if you want to remain on top.

If you are not lucky enough to work for a company that will subsidize continued training for its reps, make an investment in yourself. Even if the investment is not monetary, invest your time and energy in continual learning. Take advantage of blogs, newsletters and following sales experts online.

Identify the sales leaders in your company or industry. Find a way to speak to them or observe them in action. Understand what it is they do, but don't attempt to mimic it. Instead, personalize it. Emulate the results if not the specific actions.

Compare notes with others in your company and industry. Most good salespeople will be willing to assist others knowing that what they share comes back to help them many times over. Develop a network of fellow dedicated sales professionals with whom you can brainstorm, commiserate and even celebrate.

Join a group of salespeople in your town that meets on a regular basis. Not only can the skills you learn help your career, but the networking opportunities are wonderful. Most chambers of commerce will either be the organizers or at least know of such a group in your city. If there is nothing sales-specific available, consider Toastmasters International, as it attracts a heavy dose of sales professionals.

Read. Or in lieu of the printed word, listen to podcasts while driving in your car. Of course, if you're reading this book I may be preaching to the choir. But it's finding ways to further your sales professionalism that will set you apart from the "also-rans." Read industry magazines as well as books on sales, marketing, business, human motivation and communication.

Solicit feedback from customers and lost prospects alike. What can you do better, more of, less of? How are you perceived and is it the image you want? Without learning what is wrong or can be enhanced, the chances of improvement are minimal.

Sales professionals who are employed by companies that invest in formal sales training should take advantage of it at every possible turn. Candidly, it's not necessarily that there is something new for you to learn in every seminar offered to you. But the formality of a lecture, webinar or training session reminds you to use, implement and benefit from what you may already know.

Many sales trainers are preaching the same things. They will use original verbiage and a new twist to re-package an old idea. After all, is "needs ascertainment" any different than a "thorough discovery process?" Is a "discovery agreement" any different than a "confirmation of criteria and process?" How different is "establishing an empathetic relationship" from "lowering buyer resistance through trust?"

If you've been through Dale Carnegie, must you also master "S.P.I.N." selling techniques? If you've conquered the Myers-Briggs' four quadrant client personality profiling, do you need to also master Wilson Learning's Versatile Sales Person?

There is such a thing as overkill. What is more important than course after course is to apply the knowledge these courses seek to teach. Find out what works for you. And create a repeatable, sustainable process on which your sales career can thrive.

We had a sales person in one of our North Carolina offices who hadn't been in sales prior to joining us. She was a single mom who had beaten cancer twice. Louise placed enormous demands on our support team, but nothing more than she asked of herself and of her clients in terms of commitment.

Her success was not born stemming from the time she exited the womb. It was born of necessity and a recognition of opportunity. It resulted from a need to achieve certain levels of success and an ability to bulldoze her way towards a goal without being victimized by patience, pussyfooting or people. She'd beaten death. Why the hell would a simple sales obstacle get in her way?

Salespeople aren't born into their professions. Some sales wannabes cannot be trained. The aptitude or attitude is not inherently present in their makeup and thus cannot be developed. Sales is a set of skills and actions that when properly applied yields predictable results with varying degrees of consistency.

Sales people aren't born. They are carefully molded.

Incentives

Atlantis Resort
Paradise Island

Here is the theory: a company says if a salesperson or sales team achieves a certain level of success, they get an extra reward. By putting a "carrot" out there, it is expected that reps will stretch, push harder, work more and more effectively so they may win the prize being offered.

Some say incentives should not be cash because a commissioned rep is already earning more cash by selling more product. Besides, something tangible, memorable or experiential that can be shared by the rep's family or significant other will be more appreciated.

Also, it's human nature to brag about a trip you win, whereas that same salesperson is not going to go about bragging that they earned a specific extra cash bonus. The thinking is that those bragging rights serve as a motivator. Incentive companies will also tell you that the participatory nature of sharing an incentive prize with others will also get those "others" to help management push reps to new heights.

There are hundreds of incentive specialty firms offering to assist companies in motivating either their sales forces or even their loyal customers. Whether it is an exotic trip or a discount coupon for a beer-of-the month club, different incentives will work with different people. Finding one plan to motivate an entire staff is a challenge.

One problem is when companies set the bar too high and nobody wins. The company hopes everyone will stretch and someone will win. When nobody wins, the backlash, disappointment and damage to credibility can mean everyone loses.

Another problem with incentives is when a company says, "All reps that sell x get to go on the company cruise." Most salespeople work hard. The successful ones work particularly hard and chances are if they get time off and are awarded a cruise, their preference would *not* be to spend it with people from work.

There are times a company will utilize incentives to mask an otherwise flawed compensation plan. Wow, the company sends its top reps and a guest to an island every year. Who wouldn't want to work there? Well, let's see, the trip would actually cost $4,000 per couple. Let's say the industry average was to pay 15% of sales to its reps and this particular company only pays 12%. In other words, they are underpaid by 20% versus the industry average.

Nowadays, if one fifth of your sales income as a full-time commissioned salesperson doesn't equal more than $4,000, you need to find another product to be selling.

My father told me this story about his Uncle Ben who owned a hotel in Lynn, Massachusetts. It seemed there was a hotel telephone operator employed there for many years. Back in the 1940s, the hotel put in a switchboard and became quite progressive by having phones in all the rooms. On infrequent family visits to the Boston area we'd visit Uncle Ben. Although it was then the '60's, the switchboard was still in use and quite fun for my brother and me to play with.

The phone operator was a loyal employee. However, it seems Uncle Ben was tight with a buck. Whenever the employee would seek a raise my uncle would counter with an offer of an incentive. After some sob story about money being tight and not being able to afford raises for all the staff, he'd say, "If we go one month without any problems in our phone service, although I can't give you a raise, I'll give you a $5 bonus."

I'm sure phone service went uninterrupted for the duration, and that the bonus was gleefully received, the operator beholden to management for sharing the wealth at a time when he couldn't afford to give raises to others on the staff. But even if the raise was only .25 cents an hour, in that same month the operator would have made an extra forty to fifty dollars! Now, he'd have to wait months to ask that overly-generous Mr. Ben for a raise again.

How is your company using incentives to motivate you?

Shortly after Syndicast was bought by the Australians, they sent an Aussie to manage the company and look into further expansion in the US market. The company, which was used to being more of a distributor of other people's programming, was expanding into some "first run" ventures. Included was a made-for-syndication television movie called *Neat & Tidy*.

Mason, the Aussie, made a deal with the sales staff. If we sold the program in 90% of the US Television markets, each rep would get a trip to Australia. The sales staff worked hard. We had to overcome the fact that our company was not known as a player in the "first-run movie" market. We had to overcome the fact that our competition was selling whole libraries and we were seeking single time periods which were harder for stations to program. When 5:00 PM rolled around on the East Coast, we worked late and pursued TV Stations in the Central, Mountain and Pacific time zones. We had a goal, and it involved vacationing with kangaroos!

Champagne corks popped when we topped ninety percent. The problem with this incentive was that management was not in a position to make good on the prize, and they didn't. What did that do to morale? Their credibility? And how did it help motivate us the next time they wanted us to stretch?

Sometimes, incentives that are attained and fulfilled set an expectation that those special offers will continue in the future. Skyline set up an incentive for its reps and distributors to win a first-class trip for two to the Atlantis Resort in Paradise Island. The previous year, the trip had been to Hawaii.

Everything the company said would be provided was included – and more. There were little gifts that not only made you feel appreciated but would remind you when you were home of the good times to be had by working hard to sell their product.

Then, there was a change in management and a different type of incentive program was announced. A limited number of reps based on market sizes would win cash prizes based on sales of a particular product. The excitement of sunset in the Caribbean, of snorkeling in clear blue water, and of lavish food and drink was not matched by the chance of winning a few grand.

The reason? Reps already knew that if they sold more, they'd get more money. It didn't motivate.

It is fallacious that all sales incentives will push a staff to new heights. Some plans will work for some people.

Note to reps everywhere: always discuss the income tax consequences of non-cash awards with your accountants. If that extra amount shows up on your IRS 1040 it can play havoc with otherwise careful tax planning!

"They" Are Important

Metropolitan Club
New York, NY

I get furious when a rep's demeanor transitions from that of a competent, confident charging bulldog into a wimpy, star-struck, shrinking violet. It happens sometimes when a rep encounters "title-itis."

"Title-itis" is not a golf ball! It is a temporary medical condition evident when an otherwise rational salesperson goes gaga over the perceived station in life a particular prospect has reached.

Perhaps it results from that entire person's staff referring to the individual as "mister" even if they've worked together for fifteen years. Sometimes it's evident when the individual is a well-known person in an industry or in the community.

My problem with this phenomenon is when the rep subjugates his or herself in the process. It may go something like this:

The target client is some distance away. The rep has been trying to set an appointment with this prospect for some time. Already, the rep has met with the underlings in the company. Now, the Executive VP of Company X has communicated through their assistant that they can make fifteen minutes available in six weeks' time between 7:30 and 7:45 AM.

Running through my mind as a sales manager may be any or all of the following:

It doesn't sound as though the big time hot-shot prospect is taking the rep seriously.

Whatever time the rep has spent selling up in this company may have been wasted because the underlings clearly haven't conveyed that it would be in the company's best interest to meet with our rep.

A meeting several hours away at 7:30 AM means a half day investment in drive time plus perhaps a hotel room. Is it worth it?

Hopefully, in sales manager's school I would have learned not to be the wet blanket to a rep who is excited they've finally made it to Mr. Big! But that lesson gets tested when I ask the rep, "How come we're meeting for only fifteen minutes?" And, "Tell me about Mr. Big's expectations for the meeting?"

This is when I share this chapters' lesson with the rep. They may say something like, "Hey, this is the Executive VP of Company X. *They are important.*"

Note to reps everywhere: "they" are no more important than you. Your mindset needs to get to a place that says, "That company is damn lucky to get a few minutes of my time. If I determine I'll allow them to purchase my product, they will really be indebted to me."

"They" likely have a salary. If you are selling to a C-level executive, department manager, director, or someone with VP stripes in a well-established company, there is the strong likelihood that they have a large salary and how they spend their time on a minute to minute basis may not affect their income. You, however, as a commissioned sales rep, need to be generating a certain amount every hour or you'll be financially hurting. Nobody's time is more valuable than yours!

At some point or another in a sales rep's career they will show up for an appointment to find the person with whom they were supposed to meet has blown them off. In most cases it is an inadvertent scheduling mix-up. But it's upsetting when I hear from a rep, "It's okay, they're busy. They're important." It's clearly time to teach the lesson again!

I worked with a wonderful salesperson named Sofia Altamoretto at Group W. Originally from Italy, Sofia had come to the US in her teens. Her accent could make anything sound exotically important. She had a habit of slightly raising her voice pitch and her eyebrows when she spoke about a person and repeated their name. It made that person *sound* important.

A woman that worked for me in Greensboro also used to very deliberately say the name of a client when recounting something about the account. But, without an exotic accent, it was just a name. Everyone's got one. Understand what's important.

A few years after I graduated college, I was at a TV industry reception celebrating some award the CBS Sunday Morning News program had received. We were at the Metropolitan Club with wonderful service, great hors d'oeuvres and (most important to struggling young people starting out) free booze.

Immediately after I got in line at the bar, three men got in line behind me. At business functions, conversations are often struck up amongst strangers in buffet and beverage lines. So I turned and was greeted by famed late night comedian and talk show host David Letterman, legendary TV producer Norman Lear, and Brandon Tartikoff, the man credited with reviving NBC and turning it into a powerhouse.

When I rejoined my friends, there was some ribbing about me being the TV industry's fourth pillar of importance at the bar that evening. I distinctly remember thinking that although their bank accounts were in a different stratosphere than mine, we were just four guys all after the same thing – a refill on our drinks.

It was my personal version of that old adage – we all put on our pants one leg at a time!

Who is the most important person to your sales success? It's not the largest client you currently have. It's not the prospect you're targeting for the future. It's you.

Our Price Was Too High

Hilton Hotel
Las Vegas

O f all the topics in this book, this chapter is one of the most universal, but also unique to each reader's individual circumstances. We've all heard, "Your price is too high." Why we've heard it is the great variable.

I suggest that every sales rep in any industry practice a response to these very words. If you haven't heard it yet, you will. In fact, smart buyers are trained to feign a negative reaction even if the price quoted is significantly under what has been budgeted for the purchase.

When during your selling process should price be discussed? While there are always exceptions, if the prospect has neither the need nor desire for the product, whether your product costs one dollar or a million dollars, price becomes irrelevant.

As a rep, when your client says your price is too high, you need to be asking yourself some specific questions. First, did you qualify the prospect as to the company's financial resources or the individual buyer's ability to afford the item in question? Have you uncovered their buying motivation? Are you dealing with the person who makes money decisions?

Have you determined if their stated objection to your price is the real objection to moving forward with the deal? Or, is it the easiest brush off?

If so, is the deal salvageable and can you identify – with the help of your prospect – the true objections?

There are times a prospect may tell you the price is too high and it's actually a great buying sign! Frankly, if the prospect had no interest in pursuing a deal with you, they would either blow you off or shut you down. By stating a concern over price, they are inviting you to continue in the process.

This puts the ball back into your court. Is the price roadblock real, or is it a negotiating tactic? Can you explain the value and relative worth of your product in terms that make the initial cost discrepancy disappear when you look at a total cost of ownership?

I've adopted the "cost of ownership" argument frequently publicized by the automotive industry for use when we sell our trade show displays. There are many times our initial pricing may be higher than competitors. However, when we show the client that each time they use our exhibit they realize a saving, it starts to add up.

We go on to show a number of individual usage-related expenses a trade show exhibitor may incur. These include shipping, refurbishment, installation/dismantling, storage, asset management, and something called drayage. In fact, there have been times this approach has led to our selling new displays to people who already owned ones they thought were perfectly fine.

I have a client that sells inks. Their inks are very costly, but the amounts used are minimal. Compared to similar amounts of ink from a competitor, my client's product lasts longer. When they paint a picture in their client's minds of the numerous reorders necessary when the competition's ink is purchased, their own, more expensive ink becomes the bargain.

Some companies and some individuals are used to buying premium products. They establish a record of delivering quality products and services. Sometimes the aura of quality is reinforced by marketing tactics. You need to determine if your clients are price-sensitive or if it's not a concern (hint: while it's not necessarily a concern on some premium and super premium products or services, *nobody* likes to knowingly overpay or feel they've been taken advantage of).

Some people will voice their price concern not so much to get a lower price, but to get *something*. I'm referring to two types of buyers here. The smart buyers may know that pricing itself is fixed, but perhaps they can get better terms? Better Selections? Lower volume requirements to achieve a differing price plateau? Faster production or delivery? Increased service or training? Your job, as a salesperson, is both to know what is possible and to create value for these non-core items.

The other type of buyer who wants something may not be operating in their company's best interest. Let's face it, there are people out there who are simply pains to do business with. They may seek to turn an otherwise mutually-beneficial transaction into a pricing game. They want something just to see if they can get it.

Have you ever silently cursed the individual that set the snowball in motion in your industry that led to clients thinking about or expecting to get a discount? Who was that sales weakling that didn't create the value for the product in the first place and has now, years or generations later, left you to deal with clients arguing against your pricing. And how can you avoid being the one future generations of reps in your business will be cursing?

You, the sales rep, are at least partially responsible for whatever expectations the prospect has regarding receipt of price concessions. Did you lead them to believe the initial quote was just a starting point? Did you wink-wink, nod-nod when they asked if this was "the best you can do?"

There are countless books and blogs on pricing strategies as well as negotiation techniques. You can also take seminars and webinars or hire coaches to work specifically with your organization on this topic. Here, I'd like to share just a few strategies to help you cope when you hear, "Your price is too high." You'll need to personalize these. Smart reps will plan to encounter the situation and practice their responses for when they do.

"Other than this question of the initial price, are we in agreement the product/ service is right for you?" This sort of a comeback serves double duty. The rep is both isolating the objection and going for the close at the same time. You are putting the buyer in the position of either sharing other obstacles to the sale or revealing more about their financial decision process.

"Your concern over price is very encouraging to me and I thank you for the chance to explore the origins of your assertion." Okay, that's the pompous way of saying *"High? WTF? As compared to what?"* This approach is forcing the buyer to come clean as to the competitive situation you are in as well as if they really did have a certain price expectation, and where that expectation came from.

Let's look at an example of the sales professional who sells inground sprinkler systems. A homeowner tells you he was only expecting to pay $3,000 because that's what his neighbor paid. It's a clear path to comparing the systems and either getting them to see the value of your higher-priced system or getting them to agree to buy a product from you that is comparable to what the neighbor bought.

Also, whether you are selling something business-to-business or direct to consumers, be careful your prospect is not making a comparison to the last time they bought a similar product. Has there been a big time lapse? Has technology changed? Have the cost of raw materials or government regulations impacted the end user price?

"What's your Plan B?" Here, you are asking the buyer to share not only competitive alternatives with you, but whether the option of buying nothing is a consideration for them. If your company is competing for market share, knowing that a purchase is imminent may affect your ultimate pricing strategy on the deal.

Once, at The Exhibitor Show in Las Vegas, I was interviewing a sales rep from Chicago about the possibility of his coming to the Carolinas to work for us. With the commonality of our daily challenges it was easy to compare how we approached certain situations. The conversation turned to the how many times we'd heard the words, "Your price is too high."

Here's how he handled it. *"I have two quotes done. One is essentially the product description with a lump sum price. The other is a detailed Bill of Materials where every single piece and part has its own line item price. If they question the cost on the first quote, I simply give them a copy of the second quote and a pen. I tell them to mark out the items they don't want and that will bring the price to a lower point. Usually, they sign the contract once they get my message every piece has a cost and it's not an arbitrary game or negotiation."*

Sometimes, being direct and to the point is the best way to achieve big sales!

Great Sales Reps Make Great Sales Managers

Training Room
Skyline Displays/Eagan, MN

I once attended a sales manager's training seminar bringing together people in similar positions with similar responsibilities from around the country. John Lomen, Skyline's Training Director, was acting as the meeting facilitator as well as presenting some specific sales management techniques developed by the Wilson Learning Corporation.

Throughout three very full days of class time, along with late nights of tremendously important and enjoyable "group bonding," the one item that was agreed on was that deep inside the minds of most sales managers is a voice that says, "Why don't they just do what I did when I was selling?"

Many companies make a horrible mistake by promoting a top rep into sales management. Actually, they hurt themselves twice. First, they deny themselves the benefit of a top reps' productivity. Secondly, they presume that the individual who is promoted will have the requisite skill set to be an effective manager.

A rookie sales manager's biggest challenge when on a co-sales call with a rep is to sit quietly and observe rather than jump in and do what they had been successfully doing for years. Especially when the rep is blowing the sales call.

Why is it that so many reps aspire to be sales managers? I remember calling on WFMY-TV to sell the renewal of a TV program called *PM Magazine*. Afterward, their new local sales manager drove me to the airport. He shared how his goal was to have every rep on his staff earning more money in sales than he received as a manager. In many industries, a top rep can far out earn a manager.

Some reps become enamored with the title, with having a better office, or with the concrete evidence of career growth that comes with being promoted into management. What they need to realize is that the jobs are very different. The skills are different. And, yes, the rewards are different, too.

Sales reps enjoy seeing their clients enjoy or benefit from the product or service being sold. Managers enjoy seeing a rep develop, their numbers grow, and their competence and confidence continue to evolve.

Reps have a need to be pushing their projects through the system. Managers have a need to ensure the system is working for everyone to the benefit of the company's owners without the narrower focus on a single rep or client.

Reps balance the demands of individual clients. Managers balance the demands of individual reps, their clients, the company's ownership and the limitations of its vendors, service providers and/or manufacturing department. Reps are primarily people-focused. Managers – although they must absolutely develop, manage, encourage and assist their people – must primarily concern themselves with "process."

Reps are burdened with reports pertaining to their activities, but managers may find themselves buried in paperwork. Some managers are better with paper than people! The worst sales manager I ever had coincided with my time at Fox TV in Greenville. By all accounts, this particular GSM had been a great National Sales Manager. The majority of his dealings were with commercial spot inventory. Managing numbers and inventory was his strength. I needed someone who could manage a person – me!

Just because a salesperson is good at prospecting does not mean they will excel at monitoring the business development activities of multiple reps in disparate locations. Just because a rep is strong at closing is no guarantee that they will be strong in forecasting when they become a manager.

Successfully managing often means adapting a repeatable set of actions that are proven to work (i.e., a process), and customizing these to the unique attributes of each salesperson. If as a sales rep-turned-manager did things a certain way, he or she may not recognize the benefit in allowing for differing approaches.

A top sales rep may get the promotion because of their success. They were good, they got the job done consistently. In sales, that often means that they demanded much of themselves and didn't patiently suffer fools. That attitude and lack of patience can sometimes lead to costly errors as a manager by writing off an unproductive rep too soon instead of properly training them.

Before aspiring to climb the ladder, I urge all reps to take an inventory of what they like about their current positions and what is leading to the desire to take on management responsibilities. Be sure you thoroughly understand the tradeoff of what you'll be giving up and what you'll be taking on.

Either way, good luck and good selling!

PART 4

Selling Like
Your Career
Depends On It

The Owner Was Fired
By His Clients

Skyline Exhibits
Eagan, MN

O n the television series *The West Wing*, the President's Press Secretary/ spokesperson is a character named "CJ." During a particularly strong episode of the series, the storyline flashed back to inform viewers about the paths the characters took in their careers prior to winding up in the White House.

"CJ" had worked as a highly-paid public relations executive in Hollywood. She was summoned to her boss' office early on the morning the Golden Globe nominations were announced. A major client who was a movie producer was upset his film had been ignored by the industry. The owner of the PR firm had a choice to make. Either she fired CJ as the client was demanding, or she would lose his lucrative business.

CJ was history at this agency. She hadn't sold the press on the idea that her client's lousy film was worthy of their endorsements. Of course, this is a mythical case of a client essentially having an employee fired. What if it could happen in the real world? What if, instead of an employee, it was the boss that got fired?

Two men essentially founded Skyline Displays. Gordon Savoie, one of the founders, remained as the company's CEO until his unfortunate and untimely passing. Traditionally, he was the sales and marketing guy. The other founder, Brendan Chamblon, was an engineer who had evolved into the day-to-day management role.

For all practical purposes, Brendan was fired by his customers.

In Brendan's case, his customers were the distributors of Skyline's display and graphic products. There was discontent in the lack of direction he had for the company. People were unhappy with the pace of product development. Most of all, he was viewed as an impediment in the way of his customers growing their businesses.

A select group of the customers jointly signed a letter to Gordon demanding Brendan's removal from the company. The letter sent a clear message that failure to act would result in Skyline losing the core of its distribution network. Put simply, they'd buy their displays elsewhere.

However uncomfortable it may have been for Gordon, he recognized that without customers, there was no business. With Brendan, there would soon be no customers. Bye-bye Brendan. It took several years to finally settle the lawsuits brought by Brendan. You couldn't feel sorry for the guy. In fact, he was known throughout his customers' world for what came to be known as the "Small Brain Incident."

Brendan paid a rare visit to a Skyline training class where different members of the staff would educate field sales reps from around the world on the products and how to sell them. At one point in time, the company had relatively simple, small trade show displays. Over time, our product offerings have become larger and more complex.

In response to the developments, Skyline introduced "Project Management" teams of experts to help local reps close more of the larger projects. There was skepticism among the sales reps. Some feared they could be replaced by a corporate team. Some feared corporate might directly go after the local distributor's clients. Some simply had a concern as to how their bosses back home would figure commissions when these new project management fees were assessed.

Brendan, trying to come to the aid of the Director of the Project
Management Group in explaining the program went up to a chalkboard.
In explaining the reasons that the program was put into place, here is
what he said (keep in mind he was standing in front of a room full of his
customers, all of whom were salespeople):

First, he drew a big circle. Then he said, "This big circle is Skyline
Manufacturing. This is where the important stuff happens. Without
manufacturing, you're nothing. The only way manufacturing can do its
job properly on these big projects is to hear directly from the end user
clients without the filtering done by salespeople."

Next, he drew a circle a little smaller than Skyline's circle. "This is the
end-user customer. They're important too. They need to be able to speak
directly to the project manager. Having a salesperson as a middleman only
means things get left out or misinterpreted."

Then, he drew a tiny circle in between the two larger ones. Telling us the
tiny circle represented salespeople, he asked, "You see why it's important
not to rely on salespeople, don't you? They have small brains."

Some people who get fired deserve it. If enough customers are unhappy
with your product, service or attitude, they can fire you either by no longer
buying your product or by demanding the ownership of your company get
rid of you. These are just two more reasons why customers are the most
important key to big sales.

What The Interviewer
Wants To See And Hear

First Impressions

You've made a first impression on your recruiting executive long before your initial meeting with them. One of five things will have already occurred:

You've contacted the company in writing.

You've contacted the company via telephone.

You've contacted the company via E-Mail or an on-line portal.

Someone has recommended you to the company.

The company has contacted you either through a headhunter, or directly based on your reputation or digital profile.

The majority of positions in the sales profession are filled through one of these methods. Because electronic correspondence accelerates interaction, for many companies it has become the communication method of choice.

The downside to this phenomenon is that the art of formal business correspondence suffers more each and every day. Depending on how you view the scenario, we are grooming a nation of either functionally-illiterate communicators, or we are witnessing the continued evolution of the communications process.

If contacting a potential employer in writing (electronic or otherwise), you should make every effort to address the following items:

When possible, address correspondence to an individual, as opposed to, for instance, "To whom it may concern." In many instances, either LinkedIn or a company's website can steer you the right person. Even if you're wrong in your guess, the effort will generally be appreciated, and your application will likely be passed along to the correct hiring executive.

If responding to an ad that has called for a letter along with the resume, don't assume sending your resume alone will be enough. Some hiring agents are so frustrated with the lack of communications skills pervasive in the industry today that they simply ask you to write a letter to see if you know how. Others ask for a letter to see how you differentiate yourself from the competition – a requirement of most good salespeople. Still others ask for a letter to see if you can follow directions. Finally, you may be asked for a letter to see if you care enough about the position to write one. The lazy approach is simply clicking "Apply Now" and having a resume service forward an impersonal and inappropriate generic response.

Keeping in mind that you haven't yet met anyone at the company, this written document is their first introduction to you. It is also the first time they are judging you. Little things matter. Spelling, punctuation, grammar, neatness, complete thoughts, clarity of ideas and a specific call-to-action are all elements of how you are being evaluated.

If your written correspondence is not electronic but uses stationary and typing, be sure that neither the paper stock nor the font choice will evoke questions in the reader's mind. Don't affix any stamps promoting causes, candidates or social issues to the envelope. A US postage stamp will do just fine!

If you are sending e-mail letters and/or resumes to an employer, be sure you carefully screen your outgoing e-mails to ensure no viruses are being sent. Corporate firewalls have very sensitive screening protections that will not allow many standard attachments through. For that reason, you may be best incorporating your resume and letter into the body of an email as opposed to sending attachments. The chance of it being read by the intended party is much greater.

If your usual email signature is more appropriate for friends than it is for hiring managers, consider an alteration. Be yourself, but be your best self!

So far I've focused on written correspondence as it relates to first impressions. What about the telephone?

Of the hundreds of resumes and letters received by a company, if they decide to contact you and place a phone call to your home or cell number, what will they hear on your answering machine/voicemail? Is it anything that has the potential to offend? Even if it's in fun, is it a proper first impression to make on a potential employer? You don't know if they'll share your sense of humor or propriety.

What if you answer the phone when they call? Is the first word out of your mouth going to be, "hey," "yeah," or "what's up?" Will the tone in your voice sound as though you are exhausted or bored? Will they hear someone who mumbles?

Let's say it's now meeting time. How you look to the potential employer matters greatly. It may sound mean, and few would openly admit to something that is both politically incorrect and potentially illegal, but discrimination and prejudice is alive and well in corporate America today.

Earlier in this book, we touched on how prejudice has potential to limit a rep's income. It is also true that many companies have missed out on some outstanding sales employees because an owner or manager felt the person's ethnicity, religious beliefs, skin color or physical condition would negatively impact their sales performance.

While items such as skin color or ethnic origin are not in your control, personal attributes such as being neat or having a sloppy appearance *are* within your control. If you are overweight, be sure it is not perceived as being slovenly or unhealthy. Your clothing should be appropriate to the industry for which you are seeking to enter. When in doubt, more formal is better than less.

Be sure basic grooming is paid attention to. Your hair should be neat. Your fingernails should be appropriately maintained. Ear Wax? Nose hairs? 'Nuff said!

Beyond basic grooming and cleanliness, there is the element of how you "package" yourself, and its impact on how an employer perceives you. Remember, a good employer recognizes that the first step a prospective client takes in making a decision about buying a product is whether they have confidence in the salesperson.

Using an extreme example, unless you are selling body jewelry, chances are showing up to an interview with overblown piercings in your nose, chin, and tongue would make a negative first impression.

Examples of a less extreme nature might include wild clothing, hugely prominent or oversized jewelry, and make-up that is best saved for Halloween. If you know your tastes run flamboyant and the position you seek is more conservative, either recognize that it's not a match or tone down the personal statements.

After the very first visual interaction, before the hiring company begins to make judgments about your competence or qualifications, before they hear anything substantive from your lips, the next evaluation concerns your "presence."

"Presence" begins with nonverbal communicators including smiling, posture, and gait in your walk. Have a spring in your step. Stand tall and proud Don't frown or scowl. Do make eye contact.

Avoid wimpy handshakes. At this point in the process, you are touching the prospect, so this impression is not only mental and visual, but a physical and memorable one. Conversely, it's not a tough-guy contest. For years, people have been warned against wimpy handshakes, so some overcompensate by squeezing till bones creak.

Another aspect of your presence is the energy you bring to the interview situation. It may not be appropriate to be enthusiastic about the position until you learn more about it, but you need to be enthusiastic about learning about the opportunity!

Remember that an employer's overall perception of you starts with your physical presentation. Yes, it is shallow. It is often unfair. But it is real.

Substantive Impressions

Painting oils on a canvas has little to do with writing poetry or singing opera. Yet, all may be considered "art." In sales, the process by which vacuums are sold door to door differs greatly from the sale of international bond funds on Wall Street. However, both are sales.

For this reason, it is particularly important that readers adapt the principles, ideas and suggestions that follow to their own circumstances. As with the bulk of the preceding pages, I've tried to be general in scope, using specific examples solely for illustrative purposes.

How will you convey to the hiring executive you have prepared for the interview? The act of preparing shows that you care and invest in a selling process. In this instance, you are selling yourself. Be sure to check out a company's website and maybe the interviewer's online profile. It's okay to let the interviewer know you've done so. Have a list of questions prepared. It shows forethought.

Ask the interviewer about their background and tenure with the company. Much in the same way you'd ask a potential client about their background, people like to be given the chance to speak about themselves. Sometimes, omitting this step could be an affront to the person you are trying to impress.

Your ability to communicate effectively is being judged. Some trained interviewers will quickly eliminate candidates when they feel the person is not an effective listener or if they seem to have a hard time comprehending facts and concepts. Listen actively. Speak clearly.

Not only should your voice quality be measured (i.e. try not to shout, mumble, or drag on in a lengthy monotone), but what you say should be clearly understood, not pretentious or provocative. It is often good to provoke thoughtful answers from your interviewer, but you don't want to be seen as someone who is argumentative.

One of the reasons sales positions in some industries have such high turnover is that salespeople can sell themselves during the interview by understanding what it is an employer might want to hear. If you want to separate yourself from that pack and be seen as a substantive candidate, a good technique is to share concrete prior examples.

As in any selling situation, your prospect (the employer) has many options. Remembering the details of a specific candidate is much akin to remembering all of the features of a product. But just like a buyer might remember the benefits of product if told in story form, an employer may remember how you specifically delivered results in a past life. Make it memorable by making it real.

If the interview process is multifaceted, the potential hiring company will be watching how you interact with different levels of their personnel. It's best to assume that the receptionist's opinion of you matters as much as the president's. It is rumored that when Zappos flies prospects into Las Vegas for interviews at their headquarters, the drivers sent to pick up the prospects are formally charged with evaluating the potential hire (and some are disqualified before they ever meet the hiring party).

Are you at ease and respectful with everyone you encounter? Do you get unduly nervous with senior-level executives? Do you become flippant or arrogant when among staffers who you don't think will be judging you?

As you work your way through the process, are you providing feedback to your primary recruiting contact that you are developing an appreciation for the challenges inherent in the sales position you seek? While some companies look for experience with a certain product or industry, others specifically avoid hiring someone with ingrained habits that may be counterproductive to the company's way of doing things. It's up to you to find out what the company is looking for in terms of experience.

If they want someone with specific product or industry experience, it's probably that much easier to check you out with mutual contacts, past employers or even customers. There is a fine line between conveying an understanding of the product or industry and appearing arrogant. The former is essential. The latter is a turn-off and had better be backed up by some solid examples, references, or proof if your approach is to come on strong.

There is a balance, too, in conveying that you are ambitious and aggressive while not coming across as a short-timer who will jump at another opportunity given a chance for further growth. It's only fair to the company and to your career to be sure the growth in skills, compensation and opportunities that are realistically offered by the position are acceptable to you.

Bigger titles, special perks or expanded management roles may not be part of what the company offers. They may be looking for someone who will be happy growing their sales within a defined territory for the foreseeable future. They may be looking for someone who will be happy with new products and new prospects, and who will forego the urge to climb the corporate ladder. Conversely, some hiring managers *want* to hear that a sales prospect wants to wear the manager's hat one day. Again, it's up to you, the job-seeker, to learn what the company is looking for. It is important to convey your goals – just don't be unrealistic.

There are things that recruiters are prohibited from asking, but you can benefit from letting them know. For instance, many employers are concerned about an individual's ties to a community because they don't want to invest in training someone who is interested in relocating. Many employers are concerned with how an individual will balance their personal lives and their commitment to work.

For example, if you have young children, let the company know that you have excellent arrangements for daycare or sick child days. Turn an unasked concern in the interviewer's mind into a nonissue that demonstrates how forward thinking and responsible you are. If you've mentioned in passing that you are engaged to be married, let the interviewer know your plans are to settle and build your lives where the job is located.

Sometimes a seemingly innocent question about a spouse may not be so innocent. Hiring screeners may be trying to learn about anything from the stability of your home life to your financial situation. A rep's finances are a legitimate area of exploration.

If a position is predominantly commission-based and there is a significant ramp up time, the company will want some assurance that the prospective employee has the financial stamina to work through the lean weeks or months at the beginning of employment.

Make sure the impression you leave on the people judging you is that you take responsibility for your actions, and that if given the opportunity to join the company, you will shoulder the responsibility to bring in the revenue necessary for the company's survival, operations and growth.

<u>Questions You Need To Be Asking</u>

The one question you don't want to ask several days, weeks or months into a new sales position is, "Why did I ever get myself into this job?" Presumably, you will accept a new position with high hopes and big goals. Your employer invests in your training with the same hope that you'll perform to a certain level.

In fact, it's because a company should invest in good sales talent that you need to be leery of any organization that seems to have abnormally high turnover or appears desperate to fill an open position with a body (i.e. *anybody*).

Hiring practices and recruiting norms differ across the spectrum of sales. However, there are common aspects to the profession that anyone in search of the next rung on their career ladder should ask about. Before you open your mouth, remember to go in with the proper mindset to sell yourself.

Selling yourself must encompass all the sales rituals professionals in our business regularly employ. These include making a strong first impression, remembering the importance of non-verbal communication, and remembering "two ears-one mouth-use proportionately." If an employer checks you out online, what will they see and learn? You must be prompt, memorable, impactful and separate yourself from the competition.

You must be able to think on your feet. Contrary to popular opinion, having a plan to control the interview process is also a good thing. Your potential employer wants to see someone who can respectfully take control of a selling situation. The interview is not the time to be a shrinking violet!

Before you ask questions of the company interviewing you, it is essential to ask yourself some things:

Why are you looking for a job? Why are you considering this opportunity?

Are you in need of employment or desirous of advancing your career or income? While employers like ambition, they are skeptical of "job hoppers" who move from company to company too frequently. Ultimately, you'll need to be prepared to answer when they ask why you want *their* position. Before you're face-to-face with the hiring agent, decide if you're there to *pursue* the job or to *find out* about the job.

As one who does a lot of recruiting, I'd pay special attention to any candidate that admitted, "I have absolutely no idea if I'm right for you or if your company is the proper outlet for my skills. I'm here to learn about you and see if I can add to your success." That person makes it to round two!

Do you need this job more than this potential employer needs your skills?

There is an old saying that the best time to look for your next job is while you have one. Your objectivity may be better and the financial pressure to take something that may not be ideal is less when you're already getting a paycheck.

That same shoe on the other foot also holds true. A company should always be on the lookout for great sales talent – especially when they don't have a glaring opening that is in desperate need of being filled. This allows the company and the potential employee the luxury of time to feel comfortable with one another.

Forget about making it to round two – most applicants don't even make it to the first interview round. Often, if an applicant includes a phrase like the following in their initial query letter, they don't even make it to the initial meeting phase: "I am absolutely certain I will do an outstanding job selling your product…"

I'm all for confidence and optimism. But because most people writing such things know very little to nothing about the company, the product, or the skill sets and aptitudes required of the job, this rhetoric seems inappropriate.

Are you in this interview to impress them or to learn about them?

(These options are not mutually exclusive)

Your mindset is very important. It will guide your actions, questions, demeanor and preparation. Consider the powerful differences in these two mental approaches to an interview: first, "I really hope they like me and feel I'm worthy of consideration." Or, second, "I wonder if this company will measure up to my standards and be worthy of the time I'm taking to check them out."

From what you know of the company through its reputation, your preliminary contacts and your research, what do you have to offer them?

In hundreds of years of modern-day interviewing, the standard questions have evolved more at a snail's pace than at the speed of business innovation. There is no excuse not to be prepared to answer standard, expected questions regarding your strengths, weaknesses, or your reasons for leaving your last job.

Indeed, there are volumes already written dedicated solely to this topic. For that reason, I'll only highlight the essence of these questions: *Why should they hire you?*

Now that your head is in the right place, let's look at some questions the interviewee should ask the potential employer. Other than a cursory understanding that someone with a need for an $90,000 income isn't interviewing for a job that never has and never will pay more than $40,000, I suggest not delving deep into the money issues too soon.

If you want to make a strong impression early, as well as show respect while not ceding control, try this line: "Would you prefer to ask me some questions, or shall I begin by asking you some?" Congratulations, you now have the recruiter's attention!

When possible, when asking questions, try to avoid things that will result in "yes" or "no" answers. Remember, unlike interviewing for many other positions, your value to this employer is partially determined on their perception of how you uncover information. Don't make your questions threatening or too challenging, just phrase them in an interesting manner.

Sometimes asking a question can also be an opportunity to demonstrate something you know about the company or the industry. An example of this may be, "I've noticed that in recent months this industry sector has been soft – how is this company faring and is there anything special being done to remain competitive?

Or you may wish to show you've invested time in learning about the organization in advance of the interview. An example of this may be, "From checking out the website and speaking to some of the companies you work with, it appears your fall promotion is aimed at combating the general softness in the economy. How is that strategy panning out?"

Here is another good question to get the company to reveal what they are looking for (and to set you apart from the candidates who simply ask if they have dental coverage): "Other than *results*, can you elaborate on the different personalities, methods and procedures that separate your top reps from lesser performers?" Asked in this manner, you are acknowledging the importance of results and implying a desire to emulate the top people.

Don't just say, "Tell me about your competition." Ask, "How do you differentiate yourselves from the competition in the mind of your customers?" Your follow up once they start making declarative statements can then be, "As compared to whom?"

Now, you've learned about the competition and shown the interviewer that you recognize it's important to stand out in a prospect's mind. Also, if you are knowledgeable about the industry and the company's products, you can determine if they are full of it!

Whether the company has two employees or twenty thousand, you'll want to explore the 'corporate atmosphere' that exists. We had an employee here at the belt buckle of the bible belt that was a very devout religious man. He was frequently uncomfortable in our loose atmosphere. It's not that we were evil and he was saintly – it just wasn't a match. Some of the ways you may elicit this information include, "Do you find that certain types of people either thrive or fail to thrive in your corporate environment?" Or, "Tell me why people like to work here."

You'll want to be sure you have a thorough understanding of the company and which division of the company you'll be working for. When I first started in the tradeshow industry, The Oliver Group was the exclusive regional distributor for Skyline Exhibits and we frequently used Skyline's name in talking about ourselves. However, a prospective employee interviewing with us would want to know they are coming to work for a twenty-person company, not the larger international entity.

When I went to work for Group W TV Sales it was for a niche division called Group W Target Marketing. "Target Marketing" was a part of the TV Sales Rep Firm, which was part of the Group W Television Station Group, but separate from Group W Productions, which also had a syndication arm. Both of these entities were parts of Group W Broadcasting and Cable, which was a part of the Westinghouse Electric Corp... Find out where your position fits in!

Particularly if interviewing with a larger organization, ask about the interaction of your division with others and how the corporate mothership allocates resources for support, marketing, advertising and new product development. Find out how the fortunes of other subsidiaries have impacted your division in the past, and what is anticipated in the future.

It is fair and important to ask something along the lines of, "What are the biggest challenges facing the company at this point in time?" Not only do you want to learn about the hurdles you'll face, but you would not want to join a company if management had no understanding of the challenges they faced. Of course, when you are doing traditional selling (not selling yourself in an interview) you want to uncover the prospect's pain!

A truly thorough understanding of the company should include knowing where they came from and where they are going. Part and parcel of this is knowing what is currently delivering the revenue and profits. This will lead to your getting an education about the importance of the position they seek to fill and should lead to your asking about their plans for the company in the future.

If the company is privately held, there is nothing inappropriate in asking about the background of the owner(s), as well as the company's general state of financial soundness. In fact, if the owner is in the room, they'll probably appreciate the fact that you have an awareness of finance and fiscal responsibility.

Now that you know who owns it, how it started, how it operates and where it's going in the future, perhaps it's time to ask a bit about the products or services you'll be selling. Much in the same way you want to be sure management knows what trouble lurks on their corporate horizon, you may want to be sure they understand why people buy their products and services. Again, you want to know *and* you want to know that they know.

You will want to inquire about the customers and prospects. If they say they sell to hospitals, that could mean you'll be interacting with purchasing agents, or it could mean you'll be primarily calling on an executive on the medical staff. Which is it? Find out! Being told in an interview that a consumer product is sold to homeowners could mean you'll be interacting with well-to-do rich folks, or with people who make lower incomes. This is information you need to know.

As the interview process moves into later phases, your queries about accounts and customers should become more pointed. Are there protected or house accounts that will keep you from hitting the big numbers you seek? Will you be provided with existing accounts or will your task be entirely new business development?

Failure to ask details of how a company allocates accounts and manages territories is a sign to me that the potential hire is not attuned to sales concerns. It doesn't in and of itself signal the person isn't worthy of further consideration, it's just a flag they are not "savvy" to the legitimate concerns of professional salespeople. On the other hand, a potential hire that is overly-concerned and parses every sentence related to account assignments also raises a flag. Such an interviewee either perceives themselves to have been a "victim" of bad corporate policy in the past, or they are already scheming how to upset the apple cart.

While salespeople bring a personal style to the sales process, most companies have a process as well as procedures in place. It is important to ask about the internal procedures for several reasons.

An over burdensome bureaucracy can stymie creativity and innovation. If the reporting procedures or paperwork that are mandated become too great, valuable client contact time can be eaten away. The level of administrative support provided can greatly impact a rep's performance. Be sure to clarify if the "sales assistant" is a professional on your team or a personal secretary. Assume nothing, clarify all!

Remember that behind the positions and procedures are *people!* Ask about the staff and don't only inquire about other reps. Our small company has an incredible story to boast about when it comes to staff tenure. Recruits feel very comfortable learning that it's not a revolving door. Not only will it be important to feel comfortable with the people who you'll be working with, but they can offer you a great perspective (sometimes different than that of management) on the things that lead to success in a company. Be sure to ask if you can meet some of the staff and look for management's reaction. Hopefully, if it's a company you are interested in, they'll have nothing to hide and feel comfortable letting you talk with their people (provided, of course, that it is open knowledge the company is in recruiting mode).

It may benefit you to inquire about the company's business plan? First, if you're the kind of person who needs structure, then a whole organization that is flying without a roadmap may not be the place for you. Second, it's an opportunity to learn how the company is faring against the goals they've set for themselves. Thirdly, it leads nicely into learning about revenue quotas, advertising/marketing plans and product R&D.

Ask if the company is open to suggestions and new ideas from its staff. While few will ever say "no," if they can provide concrete examples where staff suggestions have been implemented it's a far greater sign that they'll be open to input. Early in the interview stages may not be the time to start spouting suggestions as it can be pretentious. However, using this part of your discussion to share how in a prior position an idea of yours led to greater earnings or efficiencies is perfectly appropriate!

So, now you know about the company – the people and structure, the products and procedures, the plans and requirements. You know what makes for strong reps and why others have failed. It's time to hone in on who your supervisor would be – to learn about their management style and expectations.

If a salesperson is one who may thrive when following a very structured process complete with micromanagement and detailed reporting, then that person would probably flame out in a position where the company wants to hire strong people and leave them alone to get the job done. Since you are the one devoting yourself to whatever job you choose to take, make sure there is a match between corporate and personal styles.

Inquire about the training the company provides. Be sure to explore both what is provided at the start of the employment period and what is offered on an ongoing basis. Does training go beyond the product and include sales skills? Does the company offer any tuition reimbursement or send you to seminars for skills enhancement? Is training primarily individualized and online or is it in group settings?

At this point in the process, before any discussion of money, you should be interested and or excited. Otherwise, thank them for their time and excuse yourself from further consideration. If you've made it this far through this book it may sound funny coming from me, but you need to have something other than money to excite you about the opportunity!

If the only thing of interest is the *chance* to earn a huge salary in commissions, then the likelihood you'll excel at the position and earn the gold is very small. However, if you're feeling energized and intrigued, it's time to learn about the potential rewards available when you succeed.

There is a whole range of questions regarding compensation issues that need to be explored. Remember, potential compensation may be affected by territory and restrictions on whom you can sell to, so be sure to explore both these items with the hiring manager.

Usually, very early in the process, the general nature of the compensation plan will be shared. Plain and simple, some people don't want the risk involved with working on a commission basis. Others, however, thrive in that atmosphere and enjoy knowing they will be paid based on what they produce. As there are so many variables that can go into a comp plan, I suggest asking an open-ended question to kick off that part of your discussion. Try something like, "Tell me about the comp plan and how you'll be paying me to be your new star."

Be sure all the following are clarified:

1) Base salary (if any)
2) Training/start up salary
3) Commission plan percentages and any discounts or add-ons that affect those rates
4) Draw/Advances against future commissions earned along with how and when they need to be paid back
5) Bonuses (based on your personal efforts and/or company results)?

One of the things that continues to amaze me is how many salespeople have been screwed in so many ways by companies that limit earnings either through actual compensation caps or "de facto" caps. The former says "you can earn up to "X" whereas the latter says "now that we see you've already earned "X" you don't need to have as large a territory so we're splitting your coverage area….." Beware of caps!

Explore the amount *they project* you can earn in your first through fifth years. Once they offer the amount, ask how many of their current reps are at or exceeding those levels. What have the earning trends been? Is the top rep tops because of a single home run, or because of a well thought out process and a product or service that is in high demand?

Beyond the cash portion of the compensation plan, will they be providing a car or car allowance? Mileage or gas reimbursement? Cell phone? Laptop/

Tablet? Equipping your home office? Perks (memberships, usage of company owned properties)? How are travel and entertaining reimbursed?

Be sure, too, to explore any expenses you may be responsible for (i.e. marketing or travel). Will you be paid on the gross amount of the sale, or are you paid on a percentage of an individual sale's profit? And what expenses go against that profit margin?

Finally, it's the end of the interview. You're heading for "the close" in the sales process. Have you asked for the order? Have you asked for the job? I know of several sales managers who won't hire an otherwise strong candidate because they failed to close in this selling process.

As with "real" sales, you can close using a number of techniques. For example, "Would it be better for me to start training on the first or the eighth?" "Who should I speak with regarding questions about signing up for the company insurance plan?" "Is there anything I have not addressed that is separating us from executing an employment contract?" "What is our next step in moving forward? There's money out there waiting for me to bring it to you!"

The point is, one way or another, you have to ask for the job!

Ways To Grow Your Job Into A Career

Do you have a career, or a succession of "jobs?" Is what you have also what you want? When filling out a form and it asks for the type of work you do, does what you write adequately express how you view yourself? How does the way you currently view your place in the business world mesh with where you want to be in two, five or ten years?

Maybe the next major step in your professional evolution is closer at hand? Some readers are actively looking for new positions now. Among job seekers are a mix of people who are facing varying degrees of urgency. Some are currently employed and looking for a better opportunity. Others are in-between jobs as a result of layoffs and downsizings, quitting or being fired for cause.

As you look to the next step in your job search, are you simply seeking another job to fulfill the need in your checking account, or are you carefully planning for the next rung on your career ladder?

Scream it from the rooftops. Say it loud and say it proud: "sales is a profession!" The individuals who practice this art can become and should view themselves as professionals. They help other people and companies who are in need. They provide the funding for a company's economic engine. Many are compensated on a risk/reward ratio through commissions. To sell well is to do well. When sales are low, bills don't get paid.

So, do you want to remain in this profession? Or, do you want to use it as a steppingstone to further your career? Both paths may be valid. Pick one.

As stated earlier, the most common thinking among salespeople is, "How can I get into sales management?" There are many managers who will laugh at them and pity their poor, misguided goals. Often, the move to sales management means you will no longer be doing what you like, what you're good at, and what's making you money.

If sales management is your goal, fully explore what that job entails. Talk to your own sales manager and as many other people in sales management as possible. Learn about the pressures they face, the tasks required of them and the skills necessary to successfully execute those tasks. Once you fully explore the pros and cons, it will be easier to determine if this is a path you want to pursue, whether at your current company or another.

To assist in expanding the possibilities for your career transition, let me suggest some alternate ways a salesperson may think about their skill sets:

Problem Solver

Imagine walking into a job interview somewhere and telling the recruiter "I am a professional problem solver!" The essence of sales is to understand a prospect's needs or desires and to position your product or service to meet that need. Therefore, by definition, you have a transferable skill that states you assist others in enhancing their results and efficiencies. Sure, it started as "sales," but that's not all that you do.

Coach

Chances are that people buy from you because they value your advice and respect your opinion. To achieve that level of respect, you've obviously "taught" your customers how to use the product or service and encouraged them to go about their business in a certain way. Perhaps you've shared ideas about what is working elsewhere and have devoutly cheered for their success.

Logistics Manager

Depending on what you sell or have sold in the past, there is a good chance you've worn many hats during the process. Once you made a sale, did you have any involvement with production, shipping, training or maintenance of the product? Did you have to schedule service(s) on any recurring basis? Did you ever have to deal with all of these at once on different accounts while still generating new sales and building a pipeline?

Congratulations, the circus is hiring jugglers!

Innovator

Are you the one-in-a-billion salesperson who never had to do anything creative to build a successful career? Is it true that every prospect you ever hoped to see spent lots of time anxiously awaiting your call and greeted you with check book in hand? Has every manager you've ever worked for granted every request without putting you in a position of having to sell them on the idea? All of these scenarios are common to our profession and successful salespeople have generally risen to the occasion.

So far, we've said your career path may lead you from sales into sales management. We've expanded the skills that have helped you succeed thus far from being a good salesperson to being a coach, a problem solver, a logistics manager and an innovator. See if you can utilize these skill sets to define alternative career paths.

Many sales people leave a career in sales to work for a client with whom they've established a strong relationship built upon admiration and/ or mutual respect. Sometimes that career path will be in marketing, purchasing, operations or management as opposed to direct sales. The question is, can you make a transition from being a *supplier* to an industry to a *player* in that industry?

I made that transition when I went from years of selling to television stations to working at one. I may as well have gone from working in Manhattan to working on the moon. Everything from the product, to generating leads, to support, to the corporate culture was different. So just be careful when you step out of the frying pan that you don't wind up in the fire.

Everyone reading this book is aware of the concept of networking. Not only does it help you sell more of your services and products, but it can be a godsend to assist with a career transition. You don't ever want to get a reputation in a small town or a small industry as a job hopper. In fact, the strongest networking in terms of recruiting happens when well-respected people talk to other well-respected people and your name keeps popping up as a well-respected person! Networking to help your career should not be left to when you need a job. That is the time when the people you meet may view you as in need and desperate, as opposed to on top and productive. Utilize your social media friends and connections to network. Network in your town. Network in your industry. Network among professionals and well-respected people.

It is my hope that many of you reading this book are quite happy in your chosen profession and current employment circumstance. In fact, if you can say, "I love what I do and just want to keep improving, selling more and earning more," you're now truly on the right path to big sales.

Shortly after I started with The Oliver Group, a guy named John came to our showroom. He had started a company selling computer software to small airports. John was going to attend his first trade show and needed a booth. He also needed to pay his mortgage and put food on the table, so he only had about fifty bucks to spend on the rental of a small tabletop display, which wasn't close to a going rate.

The next time John needed to rent, he splurged, and we arranged a discount so he could exhibit with a larger, albeit still plain, floor model display. After renting that one or two times, he invested in some custom graphics and eventually expanded to a twenty-foot display space. With the new larger display space at a trade show, John needed a booth that would make an impression.

We designed an exhibit that incorporated some of our newest display products and had rotating towers. Eventually, after much soul (and budget) searching, John bought the display. A few years later, John sold his company and moved to a huge house on the beach.

Another client of mine sold telecommunications equipment to cable systems. When I first started working with the company, they were two brothers and only a handful of employees. They had just moved into a small building with a workshop in an industrial park. It felt like heaven as compared to working out of their garage.

Over the years of providing them marketing assistance for their trade show needs, I watched their new office space fill up. They rented a storage space as well as a warehouse to move their production people into. Eventually, the front yard of their new building was filled with temporary trailers housing office staff. The next year I was invited to their open house at the company's new 150,000 square foot facility.

These real-life tales of seeing clients grow are examples of how a sales rep can grow their job into a career. The key is to become a valued, trusted supplier to successful people who have high ambition. Treat them right when they are stretched thin and in need, and they will remain loyal until such time as you give them a reason not to be. Grow with your clients!

Continuing a career in your current (or next) sales position brings the issue of longevity into play. Almost all salespeople experience some attrition of clients. This can result from either personnel changes or corporate takeovers at the client level or from poor quality or service rendered by the company you represent. For all these reasons, even tenured reps need to keep refilling their pipelines.

One of the best reasons to do so is to grow your income. If each year you can count on half your existing clients buying something from you, don't you want that 50% to keep on growing to be a larger number of customers? By growing your account base, you are helping make the leap from having a job to having a career.

With that growth and its accompanying tenure, you may experience a transition in the way you view yourself and are perceived by others. When you start off in sales with a company or in a given industry, the focus may be on selling. Ideally, with proper training, your mindset shifts from being a product peddler to a professional salesperson. As you earn the respect and repeat business of clientele, some may grow to see you as a valued advisor. On a career path basis, this can lead to being a consultant.

Many firms refer to their salespeople as "Consultants." Sometimes it's true and reflective of a company's approach. Sometimes it's mere hyperbole. You, as the one person most concerned with your career, can decide if you want to "consult" for your company, or go the entrepreneurial route and be a freelance consultant.

Ultimately, wherever you go next, even if it's staying where you are and only growing your bank account, getting to that destination will be the result of how well you interact with people. Above all else, while sales is a numbers game, the profession of sales is a people business.

Sell well.

About The Author

Steve Hoffman and Casper

Steve Hoffman, CTSM is the Owner and President of Skyline Exhibits & Design, Inc. Born in New York City and raised on Long Island, Steve has lived in South Carolina for the last 25 years.

Throughout his first two careers, Hoffman was involved in the sale of marketing products. After graduating from Syracuse University, he entered the television industry working for D.L. Taffner/Ltd. where program offerings ranged from popular sitcoms such as *Three's Company* to distribution in the U.S. of many British and Australian dramas, series and the skit-based comedy, *The Benny Hill Show.*

To make the transition from sales support to direct selling responsibilities, Steve moved to Syndicast Services and then on to Group W Television. As a National Account Manager for Group W's Target Marketing division, he was actively selling, distributing, developing and consulting on the local sales and implementation of station image campaigns. Projects included "For Kids' Sake," "Time To Care," "Thanks to Teachers" and "Celebrate America."

This blend of sales and marketing continued with an emphasis on TV programming and healthcare while at Medstar Communications, which was followed by his escape from the North to a short stint at the Fox Television affiliate in Greenville, SC.

Career two started by answering a newspaper ad (still saved in his desk) that was confusing as to what the job was but through some combination of necessity, confidence, skill, risk, brains and "busting his ass" has led to a successful business and career in the tradeshow industry.

Hired initially in a sales capacity for The Oliver Group/Skyline Exhibits' Greenville territory, Hoffman took on local management responsibility then added sales and/or general management responsibilities in Oliver's other four offices, eventually being named VP Sales & Marketing for the company. In 2006 Steve purchased a portion of the company and founded Skyline Exhibits & Design.

Along the journey across his two careers he has enjoyed being valued as a consultant to his clients. His years of providing sales training and opportunities to speak about sales, marketing, operations and business practices to groups ranging from manufacturers to educators, from finance to healthcare, as well as for both profit and not-for-profit entities has paved the way for his third career, where writing and public speaking are growing in prominence in his professional life.

Hoffman has two adult children. He and Ellen split their time between homes in Greenville, SC and at Lake Hartwell.

www.ingramcontent.com/pod-product-compliance
Lightning Source LLC
Chambersburg PA
CBHW020743180526
45163CB00001B/328